THE
POTATO
BOOK

THE
POTATO
BOOK

ALAN ROMANS

FRANCES LINCOLN

Frances Lincoln Limited
4 Torriano Mews
Torriano Avenue
London NW5 2RZ
www.franceslincoln.com

Designed by Caroline de Souza

Printed and bound in Singapore

ISBN 0 7112 2479 X

9 8 7 6 5 4 3 2 1

CONTENTS

POTATO GROWING

Potatoes are easy! Just throwing a seed tuber into some sort of growing medium will almost certainly produce a worthwhile crop. The following pages may disguise this basic fact. Don't be fooled.

In this book I try to cover the *c*.150 potato varieties which the enthusiastic amateur grower in the UK, Ireland and some of the nearby EU countries can obtain as reasonably healthy, certified seed to grow on. In doing so, I cover the vast majority of varieties available to eat from supermarkets, greengrocers, market stalls and farm shops. A few varieties from Europe may be missing, mainly modern salad or waxy prepack types which are found occasionally in some supermarkets. These are not always made available to the amateur grower at an early stage in their development.

Some varieties have been with us for more than 100 years and many of these are likely to be with us still after another century. I tend to classify any pre-1950 variety as 'heritage'. The next group is also fairly well 'rooted': the surviving varieties from the 'classic' 1950s through to the mid-1970s are well established, for reasons perhaps not entirely obvious to the public. These tend to have developed their commercial importance at the same time as the dominating supermarkets evolved. Not only are cautious supermarket buyers comfortable with these varieties, long established on their approved lists, but these are the most common 'free' varieties which are cheaper to grow because they are not subject to Plant Variety Rights and the control and payments which these rights entail. Modern controlled varieties come and go with depressing regularity.

While at any given time market forces lead to one or two heritage varieties changing in their availability, along with perhaps two or three of the classics, the experienced potato enthusiast can date with some accuracy a publication like this from the modern varieties available and those which have disappeared. A small number of these with useful disease resistance and decent flavour would suit the gardener, but they are eliminated because they fail to quickly find a commercial market, or have a growing characteristic that does not totally suit modern field cultivation techniques. Maintainers of varieties have to pay significant sums on a regular basis to keep their varieties protected.

Part of my own overwhelming enthusiasm for the humble spud is concerned with the insight I feel its existence gives me into the past. History is written by the victor, the academic and, above all, the person who has the time and economic freedom to write. It always covers the activities of the 'great and the good' and seldom those of people just struggling to survive. I can't help feeling that the history of the potato is often that of the survival of the ordinary human being.

I started life on an Aberdeenshire farm which grew seed potatoes, was brought up on a post-war housing scheme in a nearby village, went to secondary school and university in Aberdeen, started married life in Kincardineshire and taught biology in Angus and Fife. In other words, my entire life has been based on the east coast of Scotland where, in rural areas and market towns, the seed potato industry has an obvious presence. Many of the country people were involved in the trade because it provided seasonal jobs. As a child I picked tatties in the school holidays and later became a reasonably competent roguer of the seed crops, removing undesirable plants from seed crops before inspection. In addition, large numbers of people had vegetable gardens in which they grew potatoes that were a vital crop for family well-being, and a significant few had the secrets of how to grow pretty tubers for the many flower, fruit and vegetable shows that were an annual and important ritual of village and town life.

Potatoes were so important that they were a common topic of conversation on the Aberdeenshire omnibus or in the Montrose pub. It has always struck me as very odd that something so obviously important was ignored, taken for granted or treated as a joke by the many outsiders alienated from the production of their food. In a world where popular entertainers and less popular politicians can expect a knighthood, Archibald Findlay, who bred the three varieties of potatoes that allowed Britain to be self-sufficient in basic food requirements through two world wars, does not even rate a commemorative plaque. Some of us find it hard to see the insult in 'couch potato' or 'tattie heid'. My heroes are peasants who fed their families with potatoes when their very existence was an inconvenience to the elite; potato breeders who developed new varieties to maintain survival when the old types succumbed to disease; and the civil servants who quietly created a growing regime which allowed for the sustained production of

potatoes at a level that meant that even a crowded, industrialized island such as Britain was self-sufficient in basic cheap calories and food elements, whatever else happened.

I am intrigued by the fact that the earliest organizers of community protest could think of no worse insult to shout at those who broke solidarity than 'blackleg' and 'scab'. Could it be that potato diseases were seen as something threatening and dangerous enough to convey importance and emotion in an age when public blasphemy and other forms of swearing were unacceptable? I recently came across a modern parallel where two very religious Irish farming brothers who worked closely together in a potato-growing enterprise used the word 'Rocket' as a swear word when they wanted to express frustration. This was the worst potato variety for eating quality they had ever come across.

I know I am not going to give a balanced, broad perspective on the history of the potato. Many aspects of this history as it concerns much of the rest of the world will be missing. I am going to pander to my particular set of prejudices and, in doing so, I hope to redress the omission by others of some aspects of the story (for example, Larry Zuckerman, discussing the pivotal role of potatoes in the development of the world, dismisses Scotland merely as a place not interested in potatoes before the middle of the eighteenth century because they are not mentioned in the Bible). I hope too to shed light on why the particular choice of varieties we have exists.

HISTORY

As everyone knows, the potato came to Europe from South America in the latter half of the sixteenth century. A tiny fraction of the genetic potential of the many wild as well as domesticated species growing in South America ended up in Europe in the form we now know as *Solanum tuberosum*. Too often the role of the indigenous people is undervalued and the potato is seen as a primitive, undeveloped plant prior to this period. In fact Europe benefited from the steady selection over an incredible 8,000 years of the most useful *Solanum* genes in South America.

Solanum tuberosum has forty-eight chromosomes, as have many of the domesticated and some of the wild types of potato in South America. Once, botanists treated every geographically isolated potato population as a separate species. Now many of these forty-eight chromosome types have been renamed as subspecies of *S. tuberosum*. Some can interbreed freely while others can be persuaded to cross, with varying degrees of difficulty. All the potato *Solanum* species have chromosome numbers which are multiples of twelve. Some modern European breeding has been directed at broadening the genetic base of potatoes by incorporating 'wild' genes into new varieties. This has been very useful for introducing a few characteristics such as resistance to potato cyst nematode and some examples of blight resistance. It has had surprisingly little effect up until now on existing palatability and overall yield if measured as amount of food value produced. DNA profiling shows that many useful gene sequences were incorporated thousands of years ago. Modern high yields owe more to developed growing methods and agronomy than genetics.

The Spanish were the first Europeans to come across potatoes. They did so around 1536–8 in what is now Colombia. Their obsession with plundering precious metals is said to have hidden from them the fact that the real gold of the area was to be found in the value to posterity of these basic but highly adaptable food plants. The potato may have arrived in Spain in the 1560s. It was almost certainly of the Andean type, as these potatoes were commonly traded across the northern part of South America and were available in the markets on the Atlantic coast of Colombia, where ships called before returning to Europe. Early literature is very difficult to interpret because there is great confusion between various potatoes, sweet potatoes, yams and a host of other edible roots, tubers etc. eaten by native peoples wherever explorers and travellers found themselves. The word 'potato' is said to be derived from the Arawak Indian word *batata*, which actually means sweet potato.

Potatoes may have been cultivated in Spain as early as 1570. This date is based on interpretations of the detailed account books of the Hospital de la Sangre in Seville. These show that the hospital regularly bought what may have been home-grown potatoes in the autumn during the 1570s. The herbalist Clusius, for whom the first detailed illustrations of the potato were made around 1589, states that potatoes were established in a few Italian gardens by 1588. Clusius, Bauhin, Gerard and other herbalists had samples of live potatoes in their plant collections or pressed specimens. In 1596 Bauhin was responsible for the first detailed written description of the potato in Latin and for the name *Solanum tuberosum*. In the following year Gerard was responsible for the first detailed written account in English. These herbalists, who were the nearest thing to academic botanists of the period, get much attention in studies of the history of potatoes simply because they were the only people writing about the plants. Their work (particularly that of Gerard) can seem crude and eccentric by today's standards. The anonymous sailors who I would like to think carried the potatoes home after a long voyage do not get a mention anywhere in history.

Stories involving Drake and Raleigh bringing potatoes to England and Ireland were very common.

My primary school reading book was unequivocal about Sir Walter Raleigh being responsible for the introduction of both potatoes and tobacco to Europe. Early English literature, starting with Gerard, stated that potatoes came from Virginia or even that Sir Walter Raleigh brought them from Virginia personally. Sometimes Drake is given the credit in a rather vague way. A statue of Drake holding a potato plant, for example, was erected in Offenburg, Germany, in 1853. However, Raleigh did not go to Virginia and potatoes did not grow in North America. Drake was given potatoes in Chile in 1577 on his long round-the-world voyage but these could not have survived until his return in 1580. Modern historians therefore generally dismiss any connection between these prominent Elizabethans and potatoes. Nevertheless the convoluted writings of Redcliffe Salaman, who spent a lifetime collecting information on potatoes, leave the intriguing possibility that there is, after all, a connection involving the initial founding of the colony named Virginia. In the post-Thatcher world of diminished state involvement and increased emphasis on enterprise and our resigned acceptance of spin, we are even more likely to find the connection possible.

Sir Walter Raleigh organized and financed expeditions to Roanoak Island in what is now North Carolina. This was called Virginia after the Virgin Queen, Elizabeth, and is actually south of the modern state of Virginia. The settlement, which was close to Raleigh Bay, was called Fort Raleigh and the ambition was to create a permanent population that would develop England's first distant possession to emulate the Spanish colonies in South America. The expeditions needed money from investors, one of whom was probably John Gerard, the herbalist. Raleigh sent Thomas Hariot as his agent to the area in 1585 and arranged that he and other members of the party be left to assess it and to report back after being picked up the following year by Sir Francis

Drake, who was returning from a failed mission to intercept the fabulously rich Plate Fleet on its journey to Spain. Drake stopped off on the Colombian coast and held the port of Cartagena to ransom for 110,000 ducats by way of consolation and may well have obtained provisions as well. On this coast, Spanish ships regularly restocked with provisions, including local potatoes, before returning home and Drake and his crew had already experienced potatoes in Chile. I find it very believable that Hariot sampled potatoes on Drake's ship and delivered them to Gerard, along with examples of Virginian plants, for planting in his Holborn garden. Hariot wrote an account of the plants used in Virginia, which includes three 'roots', but none is the potato. Gerard's will shows that he gained financially from investing in the Virginian adventure.

Drake returned to Plymouth on 26 July 1586, having left Cartagena on 30 March. It has been strongly suggested that any potatoes from this source would have been unusable by late July. This is not true, because Colombian potatoes are tropical short-day-adapted plants which do not form tubers until the later summer or early autumn. Late-planted, well-sprouted potatoes would have produced at least small tubers before winter. It is even possible that material from Drake's stores could have survived until the following spring ready to be planted. Many varieties of potato left in store over summer use some of their energy to produce small, clean tubers at the end of the long shoots. This is a condition known as 'little potato'. These new tubers are capable of growing plants in the following season.

As early as 1699 it was recorded that Raleigh was directly responsible for planting potatoes from Virginia in his estate in Ireland, which was part of the extensive lands in Co. Cork given to him by Elizabeth before he lost favour. The 1693 records of the Royal Society state that Sir Robert Southwell, the then president, was aware that his grandfather had been given Virginian potatoes by Raleigh to plant in

Ireland. Raleigh is always credited as the source in early Irish folk songs and tales about potatoes.

I don't find it difficult to imagine many of the people involved in this sequence of events, having enjoyed eating potatoes, taking well-sprouted tubers from Drake's depleted stores and planting them just to see what would happen.

Nowadays the longest-running theatrical show in North Carolina is a play on Roanoak Island which speculates on the fate of the Raleigh colony, including seventeen women and nine children, who disappeared without trace sometime before 1590.

When I was helping the Waitrose chain of supermarkets introduce the 'Shetland Black' variety into their heritage range of potatoes, I discovered that many in Shetland believe that the variety was originally salvaged from a wrecked Armada ship in 1588. Salaman too suggests that an alternative explanation for the very early introduction of potatoes to Ireland is that tubers plundered from Armada wrecks 'may have been planted in scattered spots along the coasts of Kerry and Cork'.

Whatever the truth about the introduction of the potato to Europe, it was not, at first, in great use and genuine early references are obscure.

Huge changes in land tenure all over Europe from the sixteenth to the eighteenth centuries led to the displacement of a large number of people. People used to scratching a living on common land had their rights removed and had to rely more on day wages. They needed a food crop that was nutritious, easy to grow and would grow well enough on the small pieces of peripheral land available to rent. The potato, which was the only food that – along with some milk or other dairy product – gave a balanced diet, eventually fitted the bill. Grain was more expensive, needed more land and was nutritionally less useful. Milling was often controlled by landlords.

When industrialization drew people to the developing towns and cities from the mid-eighteenth century to find work, again a cheap, nutritious, non-grain food was required. The potato could be grown easily on the agricultural land that surrounded most towns. It could be stored and did not need expensive processing, and it could be cooked quickly and cheaply. This was the start of the modern age, defined, for me, as the point when potatoes became the fundamental ingredient in nearly all northern and central European 'traditional' main-course cooking.

The most desperate people, the Irish peasants, were the first Europeans to grow and eat large quantities of potatoes, sometime in the seventeenth century. It is the stuff of legend that Cromwell's slash-and-burn policy in Ireland between 1645 and 1652 was only thwarted by those who had a potato patch: the foliage and tubers underneath could never be completely destroyed by such tactics. Academics, using the written record, are more inclined to place the period of large-scale development at between 1670 and 1690. Only the extraordinary productivity and nutrition of the potato could support such a large population, albeit in very basic and precarious conditions, from 1690 to 1845, when the first potato blight struck. Historians frequently comment on the inevitability of collapse in an Ireland dependent on a single crop but, although there were a series of devastating 'minor' famines throughout this period, the fact that potatoes were grown on a large scale for at least one and a half centuries before there was complete collapse is often missed.

In the meantime, much worry was generated in England concerning the high number of inexplicably large Catholic Irishmen (brought up almost exclusively on potatoes and milk) in existence. They filled Wellington's armies (he himself was an Anglo-Irish aristocrat who hated to be called Irish). They made up the large gangs of navigators ('navvies') who dug out by hand first the canals and then the railways of rapidly developing Britain.

At the beginning of the eighteenth century Ireland had a similar population to that of England but a series of imposed laws severely restricted existing Irish trade and made economic development impossible. Self-sufficiency, based on extraordinarily expensive rented potato plots, or migration were the stark choices for many. The artificially induced misery of eighteenth-century Ireland beggars belief and only the existence of the amazing potato allowed survival until a time when wholesale migration on 'coffin' ships became possible. Even when many of the trade laws were repealed at the beginning of the nineteenth century, little changed for the majority in a devastated, demoralized country.

By the time of the great famines in 1845 and 1846, the only potato variety to be productive enough to support the large numbers dependent on the crop was a variety from Scotland called 'Lumpers'. This still exists in collections of old potato varieties propagated by official bodies such as departments of agriculture or by private individuals. The UK collection is in Edinburgh under the control of the Scottish Agricultural Science Agency (SASA). 'Lumpers' produces very large crops of big, lumpy, white tubers. Nothing illustrates the desperate determination to survive of the Irish cotter more than the eating of a plate of boiled soggy 'Lumpers'. They are disgusting!

In the eighteenth century the use of potatoes was also developing elsewhere in Europe. Antoine Augustin Parmentier, a pharmacist, had a trying time as a soldier of France during the Seven Years War. When he was captured by the Prussians he was fed on a diet consisting solely of potatoes. He thrived on them and was so struck by their palatability and nutritive value that he spent a lifetime promoting their use in France. He is remembered for presenting Louis XVI with a bouquet of potato flowers. The publicity value of the gift was greatly enhanced when Marie Antoinette wore one of them in her hair.

The grain shortages that were a major factor in bringing about the French Revolution concerned Parmentier greatly. At the point when Marie Antoinette thought that bread rioters should eat cake instead, Parmentier was trying to overcome the peasants' unwillingness to give up their biblical expectation of daily bread and be prepared to grow non-grain crops, particularly the far more productive and nutritious potato. Louis gave him a plot of land, Les Sablons, outside Paris. As the name implies, this plot was very sandy but he made his point by being able to grow respectable potato crops. Parmentier survived the Revolution and afterwards was again involved in promoting the use of the potato, this time with more success. I am told that there is a statue on a platform somewhere in the Paris Metro system of Parmentier handing a potato tuber to a very suspicious-looking peasant. Today Parmentier is remembered by various 'Parmentier' dishes and by a possibly apocryphal story that illustrates French subtlety. He is supposed to have set a very heavy guard on Les Sablons where his unpopular potatoes were growing, in order to keep out a starving mob. They became convinced that something of great value must be in the garden and stole the potatoes at night when the guard was deliberately withdrawn, and potatoes and Parmentier have been popular in France ever since.

I am intrigued by the first part of the Parmentier story. Potatoes were obviously common when he was imprisoned in Hanover sometime in the early 1760s. They were evidently very common in Bohemia by 1778 because the war fought between Prussia and Austria in that area was called the 'Potato War'. Both armies survived in entrenched conditions until winter came along. They did little fighting but spent their time stealing the many potatoes grown locally.

The north-west of England was the first part of mainland Britain where potatoes were grown in significant amounts. This was at the end of the seventeenth century, and the great Irish influence in the area is often given as the reason. The practice of releasing cattle to graze on open common ground after grain harvest must have prohibited the use of the very late-maturing potatoes of that period but there was less common land in the north-west than in other parts of England and small family farms and smallholdings existed.

There are only a few rare early references to potatoes in the rest of England, Scotland and Wales. It was not until sometime in the late eighteenth century that potatoes became common in these areas, particularly in the allotments or potato plots of labourers. More general field cultivation lagged behind until enclosure and developing markets evolved.

The famine caused by potato blight in 1845 and 1846 in Ireland and other areas all over northern Europe had an enormous effect. The spores of the fungus *Phytophthora infestans* that caused the blight arrived from America or Mexico, either in a parcel of infected tubers or perhaps carried by the prevailing wind. They thrived in the warm and wet summer weather and the growing crops quickly died off before the tubers had bulked up. Any tubers harvested quickly rotted in store. The conservative estimate is that one million Irish people died of starvation as a result of the series of blight-induced famines. At least one and a half million also migrated as a direct consequence. There are many books on the historical, political and social issues and repercussions – some of which continue today – of the Irish famine. Few of them cover the biological details accurately, few cover the fairly dire consequences of the blight elsewhere in Europe and very few of them cover the one positive consequence of the almost complete horror: it led to a large increase in effort by individuals, particularly in the USA and Scotland, to develop new potato varieties with increased blight resistance.

The first European varieties changed little over several hundred years from the original Andean types of *Solanum tuberosum* (until fairly recently called *Solanum andigenum*). As these were plants adapted to the constant short-day length of the tropics, in Europe the tubers did not bulk up until the shorter periods of daylight in later summer into autumn. Any pre-1860 description of a variety being early is only relative – it means that the variety was capable of bulking fully in August rather than in September/October. Tubers harvested in earlier months would have been picked while the foliage was still green and growing and therefore immature and low in starch.

New varieties were originally obtained by selecting spontaneous somatic variations of existing varieties or by cultivating seedlings found growing in the garden. The latter would have come from decomposed fruits which had fallen off the haulms or potato foliage during harvesting in previous seasons. As an example of the former, it is common in crops of 'Fortyfold', one of the oldest varieties still in collection, to find all-white and all-blue versions of this usually part-coloured variety.

During the eighteenth and nineteenth centuries growers became aware that varieties had a finite lifespan of between ten and thirty years. With modern knowledge we know that virus levels build up to completely destroy plant productivity. Early descriptions of 'curl', 'crinkle', 'streak' and 'degeneration' refer to leaf roll and severe mosaic virus infections, either separately or combined. Various mild mosaic viruses along with potato cyst nematode were probably common as well. As always in the history of growing potatoes, when significant problems arose, some sensible gardener or farmer was motivated enough and clever enough to find a solution. It was noticed that some new varieties selected from seed originating from a potato 'apple' had fresh vigour. We know now that this is because most potato viruses do not enter the developing seeds in the forming fruit. Many simply grew the seed from the ripe, dried potato 'apple' and selected the best from the many dozen seedlings each produced. At the beginning, this would have been a matter of choosing large, healthy-looking, self-pollinated fruits. As viral infection increased and this casual, mainly in-breeding, process continued, many new varieties lost vigour and were sterile, either lacking flowers or failing to set seed, and it became difficult to produce new varieties.

By 1854 farmer William Paterson of Dundee had spent an extraordinary £7,000 on bringing fertile varieties with good berry production from literally all over the world. He planted the different types next to each other in a damp orchard and, presumably, waited for the bees to pollinate for him. This was a deliberate attempt to breed new blight-resistant varieties, free of disease and capable of being parents of future varieties by cross-pollination. He raised the almost legendary 'Victoria' sometime between 1856 and 1863. This was seen as a particularly good variety and, because it produced strong berries, it was possibly the most used parent in potato cross-breeding of all time. Sadly 'Victoria', so important in the history of plant breeding, was not kept in the UK National Collection when a few others of the same period were. It is possible that it exists in other European collections, but research is required to confirm this.

The new homesteaders in the developing USA found potatoes very useful. They carried the varieties of their homelands with them; consequently America became a melting pot for European potatoes. There is a thriving industry in the present day of heritage varieties supposedly of this period. 'Russian Bananas', various blue potatoes and 'fingerlings' or long salad potatoes from Austria, Germany and France, all 'authentic', are on offer in the theme-park world of America. It would be interesting if DNA profiles of these were compared with those of potatoes in European collections. I suspect that the potatoes are authentic but their current names certainly are not.

In Utica, New York, the Reverend Chauncey Goodrich made a huge breakthrough. Having given up his original calling to become a market gardener and plant breeder, he produced the first genuine first early variety to reach Europe (for an explanation of types of tuber, see page 22). In 1851 he obtained, through the American consulate in Panama, a variety called 'Rough Purple Chile' (or Chili). From the self-pollinated berries of this, he raised the famous earlies progenitor 'Garnet Chile' (or Chili) in the late 1850s.

Some debate has been generated by the names involved. The potato found in Panama was the Andean type of *Solanum tuberosum* from the northern and mountainous part of South America, a short-day plant which does not develop tubers until autumn in temperate latitudes. However, the names 'Rough Purple Chile' and 'Garnet Chile' may indicate that tubers from long-day-adapted plants of the Chilean type (from much further south in the geographically isolated area of central Chile and the island of Chileo) were also to be found in the markets of Panama. The issue boils down to an argument over a very unlikely genetic variation versus a very unlikely shipping route. It is of so little importance to the scientific community nowadays that along with Paterson's 'Victoria', 'Garnet Chili' may have been lost from the main collections – although since this 'fact' was given some publicity a few years ago, there have been some unverified claims of its survival.

From the self-pollinated berries of 'Garnet Chili', Albert Bresee of Vermont raised 'Early Rose' in 1867. This vies with Paterson's 'Victoria' as the most used parent variety in late-Victorian British potato breeding. In 1878 Peter Henderson of New York produced a second early called 'Beauty of Hebron' which was also a seedling of 'Garnet Chili'. Similarly by 1875 Luther Burbank of Maine had produced the admittedly lateish variety 'Russet Burbank' from 'Garnet Chili'. This variety went on to dominate potato crops in the USA for more than 120 years. It still accounts for at least 40 per cent of American production into the twenty-first century.

Amateur potato variety breeding seemed to peter out in the USA in the 1880s but the work of Paterson and American breeders stimulated great activity in the UK, particularly in Scotland, which has lasted to the present day. There must have been a fairly efficient postal service, for new varieties crossed the Atlantic very quickly both ways. Such traffic would be illegal today.

The first truly modern, mass-market, general-purpose early maincrop, England's famous 'King Edward', has a connection with this breeding line. Though its origins are obscure, it is said to have been derived in some way from 'Beauty of Hebron' by a gardener in Northumberland in about 1902.

In 1872 another famous Scottish breeder, John Nicol of Arbroath, produced 'Champion', probably from a seedling of 'Victoria' although he was never absolutely sure. I have lost count of the number of elderly Irishmen who have told me that this was the finest variety ever grown in Ireland. The situation, as usual with anything to do with potatoes, may be a little more complicated. I recently learned that another Scottish variety, 'Buchan Beauty', was renamed 'Skerry Champion' when it reached Ireland in the 1920s or '30s and a few of the fond memories may be referring to this variety.

James Clark of Christchurch, Hampshire was a professional expert on matters horticultural and possibly one of the earliest hybridists. This was the term that plant breeders called themselves when they took isolated pollen from one parent to the stigma of a different parent, taking care to prevent self-pollination. By using such parents as 'Early Rose' and 'Victoria', he produced a significant portfolio of varieties including 'Maincrop' and 'Magnum Bonum' in 1876, 'Abundance' in 1886, and 'Ninetyfold' and 'Epicure' in 1897.

Robert Fenn of Sulhamstead, Berkshire, also raised many varieties at this time, although less is known of the parent varieties. He is often mentioned in the same breath as Clark because, between them,

they supplied the majority of the 'Sutton' varieties in the late nineteenth century. Seed suppliers Sutton & Sons were at that time based in Reading, close to both Clark and Fenn. Most of Fenn's varieties achieved no other commercial success. The exception is 'International Kidney', which was marketed through another company in 1879, possibly before Fenn became involved with Suttons. This was taken to Jersey and became known as 'Jersey Royal', and is still an important commercial crop today. This name started off as a synonym, possibly to disguise its origins, and is now an internationally protected trademark!

As a culture of potato variety breeding developed, particularly in Scotland, a dilemma arose. A great deal of time, knowledge, money and skill was involved when this was done well, but how could variety breeders benefit from their efforts in a completely unregulated market? The answer was usually that they could not. A few breeders such as Clark and Fenn took what they could get by selling the whole initial stock of a new variety to a company such as Suttons who were selling to the retail market. Generally, though, good varieties were openly or covertly taken over by commercially successful growers and merchants.

Throughout the Victorian era and up until about 1920 all good varieties received other names or synonyms. This could be done innocently. A farmer could, for example, multiply a stock of a vigorous variety that he had found as a field rogue and sell it a few years later under a new name of his choosing. Inevitably it would be an already established variety. Marketing descriptions (or even trademarks) could get confused with variety names by subsequent growers and 'International Kidney' could end up, say, as 'Farmer Brown's Pride' a few years later. New varieties produced by self-pollination could, sometimes, be very similar to the parent. The breeder would know a variety was different, might recognize subtle differences, but above all would have a new clean virus-free variety where the stock of the parent variety was badly compromised with virus etc. However, the most common reason for the existence of synonyms was to deceive customers into believing they were buying something new.

In the last half of the nineteenth century, a sophisticated potato market evolved to feed the UK, the most industrialized country in the world. Prices were high enough to maintain a network of merchants. Large mechanized farms were developed in Lincolnshire and surrounding counties. Growing techniques improved and allowed greater production.

Every year Scottish farmers who grew small crops of disease-free 'seed potato' tubers met English merchants and growers at the London Cattle Show and bargains were struck and contracts later exchanged. The postal and telegraph systems enabled quick communication and the railways allowed for fast and economic transport of the tubers. The degeneration and evolving blight described previously meant that a constant stream of new, clean varieties needed to be produced. So much money was to be made in England that, as soon as a promising new variety became available, growers and merchants in Lincolnshire and adjoining counties 'forced' seed potatoes of the variety in greenhouses. After chitting the tubers, they cut out every eye and planted them all out in separate pots to produce potato plants and then repeatedly made stem cuttings from the plants. They even left the cut-up tubers to develop weak secondary shoots to produce more stock. One merchant boasted that if he could get hold of 14lb of a variety he would, by the following year, have enough seed tubers to plant half an acre. To exploit the high health reputation of Scottish seed this English seed produced a year later would be sold as 'once-grown Scotch seed'. In subsequent years this stock would quickly gain virus in the mild growing conditions of the south.

Between 1900 and 1904 a classic market bubble developed, with 'in' varieties fetching huge sums and housewives, grocers and dentists speculating like mad, particularly with small amounts of 'Northern Star' and 'Eldorado'. These were sold at the very peak of the market for more than their own weight in gold.

The rapid growth of the bubble was, to a large extent, fuelled by the activities of the great Fife potato breeder Archibald Findlay of Mairsland Farm, Auchtermuchty. He bred an unequalled line of varieties. These included 'British Queen' and 'Up to Date', which were the leading varieties at the beginning of the twentieth century, and 'Majestic', which was said to have accounted for 60 per cent of the UK's production for 60 per cent of the century.

Findlay helped develop the concept of a seed potato industry and was extraordinarily enterprising. In the 1880s and 1890s, he invited the largest growers in Scotland and England to visit his growing crops in Fife. The trains stopped at a small station near the crops, horse-drawn brakes were provided and, after a trip round the fields, the party retired to a hotel for lunch and seed orders were taken. Findlay's seed potatoes were also sent by clipper ship for immediate planting in New Zealand. He travelled all over Britain by train to promote his varieties at talks for farmers and merchants and to trade in his potatoes at markets. He became very frustrated at the huge profits that English once-grown stock of his varieties were providing for others and continually preached that farmers should be prepared to pay a little more for his cleaner material direct from the lower-yielding, hilly fields of Scotland.

The son of a village grocer, Findlay started growing on rented land and then, with great difficulty, bought his own small marginal farm. He developed many growing and storing techniques which were the precursors of some of today's practices. It is clear from his writings that he was a hybridist and understood flower structure, and the photographs of his homes always show a large conservatory or greenhouse. He was well aware of the necessity to promote himself and his product, and he left his appreciative audiences in awe of his achievements by telling them a great deal of accurate plant science without revealing too many details of his process of breeding and selection. He would give broad details of cross-pollination and say that all his varieties had the 'blood' of Paterson's 'Victoria' in their breeding lines, but he always left out the details of actual parents.

After a string of minor successes, his variety 'Up to Date' hit the international big time in the late 1890s and was exported as seed all over the world, starting the international Scottish seed potato trade. Others profited far more than he did and consequently he stated that he was very unwilling to sell the varieties that came after 'Dates' until he had had time to build up large stocks. Farmers and merchants who had dealt with him for years put great pressure on him and he relented enough to sell small trial packs at what he thought were very high prices. He was fairly annoyed that this fuelled the market bubble instead, particularly with his varieties 'Northern Star' and 'Eldorado'. It has to be said that some of the variety names he hit upon at this stage such as 'Millionmaker', 'Diamond Reef' and, of course, 'Eldorado' did little to slow demand.

He decided to short-circuit the whole system by taking out a large bank loan to buy a Lincolnshire farm, Langholme Manor, near a railway station in order to grow and sell directly his own unforced 'once-grown Scotch seed'. The short time he spent there was miserable. First he had flooding problems. Then, worst of all, a merchant became convinced that 'Eldorado' already existed 'amongst' stock of an earlier variety called 'Evergood'. By this, presumably he meant that it was a spontaneous genetic variation. In his own literature, public and private, Findlay always treated 'Evergood' and 'Eldorado' separately. 'Eldorado' was described as being similar to 'Evergood' but with a slightly longer, narrower tuber

and a much stronger flower. Findlay's secrecy about the origins of his varieties backfired. The merchant, Mr Kime, at some expense published an advertisement in the Lincolnshire agricultural newspapers condemning 'Eldorado' and released all his customers from their purchase contracts, expressing a willingness to refund deposits. The whole bubble burst as quickly as the recent dotcom fiasco. Findlay lost his large farm and returned home to Fife to a quieter life with a damaged reputation. 'Majestic' was still to come but Findlay was by this time as interested in his feud with the local town Provost as he was in potatoes.

Other breeders of note at this time included William Sim of Fyvie, Aberdeenshire, who produced 'Duke of York', which was initially marketed by Daniel Bros of Norwich before becoming generally popular across Europe. It became 'Eersteling' in the Netherlands. Like Findlay, Sim was also interested in cattle breeding and in producing new varieties of other plant crops. There was a strong concept of 'pedigree' breeding involved in all these activities. Charles Sharpe of Sleaford produced 'Sharpe's Express', 'Sharpe's Victor' and others. There is some doubt among the local historians of modern Sleaford as to whether he did the actual crossing and selection himself, because he ran a very large milling and seed merchant concern and may well have employed staff to do this work.

The most respected breeder of this time and well into the twentieth century was undoubtedly Donald Mackelvie of Lamlash, Isle of Arran, who produced the large portfolio of 'Arran' varieties. He was a bachelor and owned a general merchant's business and some land. Consequently, he was under far less pressure than Findlay to succeed financially. He developed very good relationships with the officials of the developing bureaucracy that was steadily taking overall control of potato production in Britain. He concentrated on developing the skills of selection. He did some of his own crossing but many of his most successful varieties were derived from the seed produced for him by Mr Keay of Merry Hill, Wolverhampton.

'Arran Consul' is possibly the best keeping potato of all time. It was grown by special arrangement during the Second World War to ensure supply during April and May. 'Arran Pilot' is still, by some margin, the most popular garden variety in the UK because of its fine cooking qualities and flavour. Its complete lack of uniform size and shape led long ago to its demise as a commercial crop. The same 'Arran Pilot' plant, at maturity, will produce everything from small, almost round tubers to very large cigar-shaped tubers. It is hard to understand why the key people in the modern ware (eating potato) industry are so convinced that flavour is not an issue with customers when 'Arran Pilot' has been in high demand for so long by the gardening consumer, who has complete control over his variety choice. Unlike Findlay, Mackelvie received several awards and some recognition for his achievements during his lifetime.

I have had the privilege of being deeply involved in the revival of interest in potato varieties old and new that has occurred in recent years. At potato events and vegetable shows, whether working on my own or with the gentlemen of the Three Countries Potato Group (Guinness world record holders for the number of potato varieties displayed at a potato event), I have gained an insight into the importance of potato breeding in the past. I am regularly offered tubers of family heirloom varieties which are probably not in any official national collection. It is clear that as well as the relatively successful breeders there were hundreds of enthusiastic amateur breeders around. A tiny number of their varieties have survived against the odds and have been grown by succeeding generations of family or family friends.

In 1968 the Potato Marketing Board produced an index of potato varieties introduced to Great Britain in the late nineteenth and early twentieth centuries. This was very far from being a complete list but 65 per cent of the varieties concerned had been bred by Scots. If market impact had been measured the figure would have been much greater. This amount of breeding activity and the clean growing conditions are the prime reasons for the Scottish seed industry coming into existence.

In 1918 the first government seed potato certification scheme in the world to regulate standards was established in Scotland and the inspections of growing crops were initially free. By 1920 the Department of Agriculture was charging two shillings per acre.

The showing of potatoes started in mid-Victorian times. There is a persistent but unconfirmed story that the first items ever shown by the Royal Horticultural Society were potatoes. The efficient and cheap postal service of the time allowed the development of several mail-order catalogues featuring potatoes. The list includes those of Sutton & Sons of Reading, Messrs Dobbie and Co. of Edinburgh, Daniel Bros of Norwich, Webbs in the Midlands and James Carter and Co. of London, as well as many others. These names have echoes in the companies still around today. One catalogue (that of B.K. Bliss and Sons) claimed to have 500 different varieties. These companies feature strongly in the record because their catalogues were printed by the million every year. They were in the business of self-promotion and the catalogues add hugely to the confusion that existed over the potato varieties of that time. As well as the synonyms which developed in the agricultural world, many were added in seed catalogues to give the impression that the companies supported a huge breeding, trials and development programme of their own. A few did have potato trials or demonstration plots and a few gave some money to the real breeders to obtain initial use of the variety. As mentioned already, this was the only way an independent breeder could obtain any financial return for his efforts. I say 'his' advisedly, as I know of only one woman involved, Miss King of Mount Mellick, Ireland, who sold 'Flourball' to Suttons in 1895.

In 1916 the Royal Horticultural Society set up a committee to grapple with the problem of the profusion of synonyms. This proved to be too great a task and in 1919 their work was taken over by the Synonym Committee formed by the National Institute of Agricultural Botany in Cambridge (NIAB) and the Board of Agriculture in Scotland. Their remit was to assess all known varieties in terms of all foliar, flower and tuber characteristics, maturity type, yield, disease resistance and known history, and decide if they were genuine varieties or synonyms of already existing varieties. (A wide knowledge of variety characteristics still exists in Scotland to this day and is perpetuated every year in a number of courses for the training of new crop inspectors and roguers.)

It was quietly admitted at the time of the Synonym Committee that there would be a few genuine varieties raised from seed whose characteristics would coincide to a large extent with an existing variety. When such varieties were declared to be synonyms, it caused great offence to the genuine breeder, but the committee continued undaunted with crusading zeal under the chairmanship, from 1920, of the unstoppable Redcliffe Salaman. It was a case of necessity because the seed catalogues, merchants and unscrupulous growers had created a situation of chaos. The three most extreme examples were 'Up to Date', which was officially said to have over 200 synonyms, 'Abundance', with over 100, and 'British Queen', with 75, and there were very many others. Suttons had paid Clark for 'Abundance' and it was most commonly known as 'Sutton's Abundance'. Other catalogue companies simply wanted the variety but did not want to acknowledge the role of their rival.

Findlay's varieties, being among the most commercially successful in the world, were found to have large numbers of synonyms. Again his secrecy and talent for self-promotion backfired and somehow he was seen as a major player in the synonym game. A large number of his varieties were declared to be synonyms of previous varieties and, despite the existence of a substantial body of undisputed Findlay varieties, his reputation plummeted irredeemably for the second time, particularly in England. He was and still is a great hero of the handful of families who have a long traditional link with the commercial side of Scottish seed industry. Rather obviously from the amount of space I have given him, it is my opinion that he was more sinned against than sinning. He did not deliberately create the potato boom and I think many of his synonymous varieties had been raised from seed or were seen by him as genuine genetic variations.

Other historically important individual breeders should be mentioned at this stage. K.L. de Vries bred 'Bintje' in the Netherlands in 1910. This still dominates growing in Holland, Belgium and northern France. It has a similar reputation to that of 'King Edward' in England. It is possibly the most general-purpose variety of all for it holds together quite well but has high enough dry matter to be the most common variety used to make fresh and frozen chips in that part of the world. In the UK we eat huge amounts for most of the supermarket own-brand and catering-company frozen chips are produced in Holland or Belgium.

Dr J.H. Wilson, who was responsible for the development of St Andrews University Botanical Garden, bred several varieties, one of which is still available. This is 'The Bishop' which is only obtainable now as a microplant (see page 29) but is thought to be one of the best long (kidney) exhibition types ever.

John Watson, plant breeder for McGill & Smith of Ayr, bred the successful 'Doon' series. Ironically the only one of these still available is 'Ballydoon', which was never a commercial success but is greatly valued by enthusiasts for its eating quality. McGill & Smith's most famous variety was 'Home Guard', produced during the Second World War and promoted by members of the Home Guard. It quickly became Britain's most important first early because of reliable high yield. It is still the most important first early in Ireland. It was not bred by John Watson and there are many claims in Angus and Perthshire of involvement in its breeding or promotion. One source states that it was 'selected by Mr Howie of Glencarse'.

Charles T. Spence of Dunbar bred the 'Dunbar' series. Of these, 'Dunbar Rover' and 'Dunbar Standard' are just about still available.

James Henry of Cornhill, Banffshire, was said to have unwittingly left a fortune in a storage pit when he emigrated to Canada. His new variety was named 'Kerr's Pink' by the merchant who bought the stock. It was and still is the most popular potato in the north of Scotland. More impressively, it is still the most popular variety in all Ireland to this day. Plant Variety Rights did not exist then and Mr Henry would have found it very difficult to successfully exploit his floury pink. Once it was released anyone could grow it. By becoming Canada's most successful agricultural journalist, he probably did more for his family's financial security than he could have done by potato breeding.

John Clarke of Mosside, Co. Antrim, Northern Ireland, produced the 'Ulster' series. He started in the age of the individual breeder but was still producing successful varieties well into the age of state-sponsored plant breeding. He illustrates well one of the conclusions that must be drawn from a study of potato breeding through the ages: the main skill is that of being able to select a worthwhile new variety from the hundreds of seedlings each cross produces. Individual flair seems far more adept at this than the considerations of a committee or group.

State-funded plant breeding was seen as a natural development as the Scientific Civil Service evolved. The synonym situation, the need for independent seed certification, the difficulties plant breeders had in generating income and the need for a central strategy to provide enough potatoes in time of war had provided enough social pressure to make centralized control of most matters concerning potatoes in Britain acceptable. The increasing occurrence of a very nasty disease called wart disease (*Synchytrium endobioticum*) made this even more desirable. This fungal disease produces very unpleasant cauliflower-like growths on tubers and stem bases. Infected crops quickly rot and infection remains in the soil for very many years. Legislation was introduced to schedule every contaminated field in the UK and ban susceptible potatoes from these. Testing procedures were developed, immune varieties were identified and all new varieties produced had, in practice anyway, to be immune. The numbers of private British potato breeders declined rapidly as the whole process was seen as being too science-based for individuals to contemplate.

The varieties still available today produced by the state-funded breeding programmes of the Scottish Plant Breeding Station (Pentlandfield, Edinburgh), Maris Lane (Cambridge), Loughhall (Northern Ireland), Oak Park Breeding Centre (Carlow, Eire) and the Scottish Crop Research Institute (SCRI) are covered in the potato guide on pages 38–126. At the moment the Irish varieties of TEAGASC of Oak Park are the most successful from still existing state-funded enterprises. Maris Lane was sold off and became the commercial company PBI Cambridge. At present it is Cygnet PB. Pentlandfield activities were reduced and transferred to the Scottish Crop Research Institute. Oak Park in Ireland and the Northern Ireland Plant Breeding Station still exist in some form of state ownership.

Some universities round the world have also become involved in potato breeding, usually where individual staff have developed an enthusiasm within appropriate departments or where state funding has been strategically directed.

What was the Soviet Union grew one third of the world's potato crop and, in the Soviet bloc, a huge effort was made to improve existing varieties. A large collection of *Solanum* species, subspecies and varieties was painstakingly gathered from 1925 to 1933 by Vavilov's Russian expeditions to South and Central America. During the Second World War scientists at a breeding station outside Leningrad made incredible efforts to save the tubers from the collected plants for future breeding programmes. They risked being killed by German shells to collect the small tubers from their plots and then carried them all the way into the besieged city to survive the fierce winter weather. They suffered near starvation and burned nearly everything flammable in the building for heating to ensure that the precious tubers survived.

The Netherlands has dominated potato breeding in Europe in the latter part of the twentieth century. J.P. Dijkshuis bred 'Record', 'Estima' and 'Penta' while J.P.G. Könst produced 'Wilja', 'Cosmos', 'Marfona', 'Ausonia', 'Kondor', 'Fianna' and 'Concorde'. They, and many other Dutch 'hobby' breeders, were supported by their agricultural cooperatives or potato companies when international Plant Variety Rights were introduced in the 1970s. These rights generate payments in the form of royalties paid by growers and give the individuals, organizations or companies who own modern varieties control over what can be done with them (in the UK they lapse after thirty years). The existence of the rights led quickly to the development of vertically integrated potato organizations in the Netherlands, each with their own economically important portfolios of varieties. They developed in a country with huge expertise in crop production and with top-quality land at the transport hub of Europe. They generated income at every stage of production, packing and even some processing and quickly dominated seed and ware production in Europe and much elsewhere, including the production of seed in Scotland and both parts of Ireland.

Dr Jack Dunnett in Scotland noticed that this was happening and in 1975 left the Pentlandfield Plant Breeding Station, where he had helped produce the 'Pentland' series. 'Pentland Javelin' was his most successful variety of this period. He disagreed with the long-term strategy of the new director and felt that there was once again a place for individual flair in a world of plant breeding now protected by Plant Variety Rights. At a time when the state programme in Scotland has not produced a true commercial success since 1970, Dr Dunnett, as part of his own potato company, has gone on to become the modern equivalent of Archibald Findlay with a dozen or so commercially significant 'Caithness' varieties. Like Findlay, he is a great believer in developing pedigree lines. The number of his varieties in this guide is a testimony to his success against the odds.

The International Potato Centre in Lima, Peru, has its own research programmes and gives advice to Third World countries about developing their potato-growing industries. It was set up with international funding and part of its remit is to save what is left of the rapidly disappearing spectrum of wild and domesticated potato species, subspecies and traditional varieties to be found in South America. Environmental pressures on delicate habitats and economic pressures on farmers to drop old traditional forms of potato in favour of modern varieties do not make this easy. Conventional breeders in various institutions around the world are still striving to produce a 'super spud' by patiently carrying out multiple crossings of various collection or only part-wild domesticated plants with existing varieties in the hope of obtaining a high-food-value potato which will grow in less than perfect conditions and show long-term multiple disease resistance. This is a very long-term strategy. They are still using the descendants of plants, seeds or tubers collected by the Vavilov Soviet expeditions to South America from 1925 to 1933 as well as those available from, for instance, the International Potato Centre or the British Commonwealth Collection at SCRI Dundee. Up until now short-term 'pedigree line' breeding, which involves crossing already successful varieties (with only the occasional strategic use of 'wild' collection material), has been far more successful than state-funded long-term breeding. In the history of potatoes there have always been exceptions to every rule and I have a slight suspicion that some long-term projects may produce something of note in the near future. I am particularly interested in the varieties produced by the remarkable Sarvari family in Hungary. For many decades they have worked on producing material within the pan-Soviet plant-breeding programme and then continued against the odds as a family concern after the fall of communism. Their genetically sophisticated breeding crosses are very disease resistant. With some Western interest now involved some of their varieties are just starting to appear.

Genetically modified (GM) potato varieties, where 'alien' DNA from outside the *Solanum* genus is introduced by genetic engineering techniques, are the hope for the future, according to those with the facilities to produce the material. An application for grant funding based on a programme of genetic modification is far more likely to impress both state and commercial purse holders than a conventional breeding project. They are impressed by the use of 'new' science and the relatively short timetable involved. Large claims have been made about a new future with GM potatoes providing food for the world. However, I find it odd that most of the activity in this area has involved the 'Russet Burbank' variety of 1875,

which is the foundation of most of the American potato processing industry but not the most productive variety in the world and very disease susceptible. I suspect that modified versions of 'Russet Burbank' would be eligible for Plant Variety Rights and gene patent controls and would generate large royalty payments. As usual money and not idealism is the driving force.

Moreover, it is by no means certain that genetic modification will be successful. Historically, disease resistance in potatoes based on a single gene has always been overcome by the mutation of the disease organism. Long-term resistance has usually been based on the activities of many genes working at several sites on more than one chromosome. So far most GM examples involve single short pieces of DNA.

In Europe, there is also great public suspicion of genetic modification. There is much awareness of the consequences of BSE. This disease of cattle was caused by a rogue self-replicating protein – a prion – possibly passed on in feed containing processed cow offal. Before the outbreak the vast majority of biologists did not even know that prions existed. A long list of other agricultural, environmental and disease disasters in recent decades has added to the general concern in Europe about the industrialization of the food chain. This has left the public almost instinctively very wary of the unseen consequences of combining bits of DNA that have been, up to now, kept separate by the results of millions of years of evolution. It is difficult to imagine GM varieties having a future in this part of the world. Possibly pharmaceutical chemicals could be produced in GM potatoes somehow kept out of the human food chain. Possibly complexes of actual *Solanum* genes from species that won't cross with *S. tuberosum* will eventually be introduced using GM techniques. It would require a European political climate very different from that of the present for that to happen.

SEED POTATOES

These can be divided into four categories (planted March–May, that is in spring once all danger of frost is over in an area):

FIRST EARLIES – Ready June to July (even earlier in some sheltered coastal areas which are frost free early in the year). Sometimes described as ready 10+ weeks from planting.

SECOND EARLIES – Ready July to August. Sometimes described as ready 13+ weeks from planting.

EARLY MAINCROPS – Ready August. Sometimes described as ready 15+ weeks from planting.

LATE MAINCROPS – Ready September onwards. Sometimes described as ready 20+ weeks from planting.

It is difficult to be precise about timing. Much depends on whether the tuber has broken dormancy, what the initial soil temperature is and what growing conditions are like later. It is important to note that the strict terminology is based on natural senescence (die-back) time. Many catalogues make the mistake of saying a variety can be used as, say, a first early when they mean that it has become common practice to use the potato in an immature state, harvested while the plant is still green and still growing.

Seed potatoes can only be produced for sale in fields tested and shown to be free of potato cyst nematode and which have not had a potato crop for several years. Details of certification schemes are fairly complex and vary from one country to another. Basically seed potatoes start off as completely disease-free stock (for example, as laboratory-grown microplants that produce mini-tubers in a soil-free environment) and go through a

sequential scheme where every year of subsequent field growing leads to a slightly lower grading. Inspectors look at crops systematically and judge any visual symptoms of disorders against set criteria. Depending on the results of their counts, they will award the grade applied for, downgrade or fail a crop.

There are three EU grades of seed potatoes, which we in the UK call EEC1, EEC2 and EEC3. Many countries, including the UK, have their own established grades of potatoes as well.

EEC1 – The disease tolerances are 0.5 per cent virus, 0 per cent blackleg and 0.5 per cent rots. The two UK grades VTSC1 and VTSC2 are superior to this and are also certified EEC1.

EEC2 – The disease tolerances are 0.5 per cent virus, 0.5 per cent blackleg and 0.5 per cent rots. The six UK grades Super Elite 1, 2 and 3 and Elite 1, 2 and 3 are superior to this and are also certified EEC2.

EEC3 – The disease tolerances are 1 per cent virus, 1 per cent blackleg and 0.5 per cent rots. The UK grade AA is also certified EEC3.

English CC is lower and does not qualify for EU grading. It can only be used in very limited circumstances.

When buying seed potatoes, check the label. It should be an EU plant passport with lots of details. The best seed potatoes generally available to gardeners are cool-stored Scottish EEC2. A little EEC3 is used but in general CC is used only when higher grades are not available or cost is an issue. Be very suspicious if labels are not present or if the label claims to be a worldwide passport (there is no such thing). Unfortunately labels do not give details of storage history and it is very common practice for large multiple outlets to have all their variety nets labelled with the 'catch-all' grade of EEC3. This is legal and means that all labels can be preprinted to save on the amount of detail harassed pack-house staff have to enter on the variable part of the label which is printed on site.

Seed potatoes are also inspected and compared against set criteria when graded and packed.

Saving money on seed is, in most cases, short-sighted. Low grades, commercial ware and, worst of all, garden-grown tubers carry more spores of bacterial and fungal pests than high grades. Non-certified seed will, in many cases, carry the dreaded yellow or white potato cyst nematode. Commercial ware will often have been treated with the very effective sprout suppressant CIPC, which prevents the potatoes germinating and becoming soft in store. It also prevents the tuber germinating effectively if planted later as a 'seed' potato.

VARIETY CHOICE

The choice of seed potatoes available through large retail outlets handling gardening supplies is becoming very limited. Retailers make more money from higher-priced items which take up less space. To counteract this, a few independent garden centres, potato events run by gardening groups such as the Henry Doubleday Research Association (HDRA) and mail-order catalogues have become increasingly interested in a wider range. When mail costs shot up (along with many other items) in the oil crisis years of the inflationary 1970s, many catalogues dropped seed potatoes or severely curtailed their interest. Only in recent times has this trend reversed. Indeed for choice of variety in mail order we are returning to a situation reminiscent of that in late-Victorian times, with far more genuine information, less hyperbole and far fewer examples of fraudulent presentation. Packaging and postage are still large cost factors in the price but a majority of the 150 varieties covered in the potato guide on pages 38–114 are available somewhere.

In general, 'heritage' varieties (pre-1950) have survived because of their fine flavour or good cooking qualities. My personal opinion is that the only exception is 'Majestic', which I think makes poor eating. Many obviously disagree: it dominated growing for much of the twentieth century and many gardeners are very attached to it. A limited number of modern varieties happen to have good flavour (in my opinion) but this seems to be a matter of chance. Modern varieties are inherently more expensive because they are subject to Plant Variety Rights and the payments these entail. In between are the 'classics' developed in the post-war years up to 1972, which are not subject to Plant Variety Rights and still dominate all markets, including amateur gardening sales. For more guidance on variety choice, see pages 38–114.

CHITTING

This is the process which allows strong green chits (shoots) to develop on the seed potato tuber before planting. Dormant or just-sprouted tubers are set up in trays with the sprout end (rose end) upwards in a light, frost-free area such as the windowsill of an unheated room. The warmer the room the quicker the process. It is firmly established gardening lore that chitting is essential, particularly for earlies. It gives the potato a quicker start and crops will be of usable size slightly earlier. The full situation is more complex, however, and the technical trade description of chitting as 'premature ageing' gives some indication of this. Chitting speeds things up at the beginning but it also speeds up the onset of senescence and potential yield is reduced. If the tubers are firm and still dormant when you buy them, it is possible to make a judgment about how many of them to speed up. Furthermore if you encourage apical dominance after chitting by

23

removing all side shoots and just leaving the rose-end sprouts, fewer but larger tubers will be produced. If you leave the tubers with all shoots sprouted and plant them on their sides, more numerous but smaller tubers will result.

The main message, though, is simple: chitting is not essential. It can bring crops forward but warm soil temperature at planting time can make a greater difference in this respect.

If you buy tubers of varieties with poor dormancy which have already sprouted, it is best to set them up in light as if to chit. The shoots will limit their growth and turn green and robust. If left in low light they will grow very long and be easily damaged. Often these sprouted tubers have their appearance 'improved' by the removal of the sprouts, particularly in warm retail outlets. With vigorous varieties this probably makes little difference but in some cases it reduces yield.

PLANTING

Potato growing reflects life: it is the product of a number of compromises. Purchasing reasonably high-grade seed, organizing a three- or four-year garden rotation, purchasing reasonable tools and fertilizer, and making some physical effort result in a worthwhile crop. It is possible to expand any of the elements – for instance, showbench enthusiasts will only grow in expensive, disease-free, peat-based compost and go to great lengths to obtain sought-after varieties.

ROTATION

Potatoes are susceptible to a fairly wide range of minor pests and one or two major ones (see pages 29–37). Reasonable rotation of crops in the garden is important to keep the pest numbers down to manageable levels. Pests specific to potatoes have a limited survival time if they cannot get at potatoes.

The standard three-course rotation of potatoes being followed by brassicas and then all other vegetable crops is barely adequate, even if all left-in-ground keeper potatoes are weeded out in the second year. The organic four-course, which extends the basic rotation by inserting legumes between the potatoes and brassicas, is an improvement. If space allows, quality will be improved if you can find ways to extend rotations even more.

SOIL PREPARATION

This depends on the condition of your soil and on your physical abilities. Yes, ideally, potatoes like well-dug, deep soil, with a fine tilth and plenty of well-rotted organic matter incorporated. I recommend this for anyone who is fit and has a heavy soil. Traditionally the potato plot was cleared and dug over in autumn or winter with loads of manure incorporated. Frost broke the soil structure down so that tubers could be simply and quickly dibbled in in spring, usually on Good Friday (the only spring holiday many had).

Alternatively instead of preparing the whole bed you can dig trenches at spade depth in spring and fill the bottom with the weeds along with fertilizer (high potash), manure, compost, seaweed or wilted comfrey leaves. Then add some soil before placing the tubers in the trenches and covering them. Loosening the soil with a fork either side of the trench leaves it ready for earthing up (see page 26) as the plants emerge and grow. Some even advocate autumn or winter digging followed by spring trenching.

There are easier ways. Simply placing the tubers on the ground surface with compost and covering with a thick layer of mulch, such as straw, works. The drawback is that this allows easier access to the crop for slugs and mice as well as the gardener. Nowadays I exploit the benefits of my light, sandy loam, which has been cultivated organically for at least 200 years, and do very little digging. Harvesting potatoes involves all the digging I'm prepared to do. At planting, I make an easy scrape along the ground, deep enough to hold some compost and the surrounding weeds, place the tubers on top in direct contact and cover with soil. If you use proprietary, concentrated organic fertilizers or of course chemical fertilizers instead of compost, you should separate them from direct contact with the tubers. I sometimes use a trowel to place the tubers at a deeper level under the compost. With this method, loosening the soil either side is particularly important to create enough soil to earth up. On one occasion, I had time only to place the tubers in lines on the weedy garden surface and spade a bit of earth from the side over them. When I had more time later I spread some compost over the area and tidied up the drills with a rake. I got a crop.

Deep beds have become very popular in gardens. They involve a great deal of initial work in building up frameworks to contain the beds, filling the beds with extra topsoil and creating the surrounding paths. Vegetables are planted from the paths and plants are packed in very close together. Potatoes do well in them. This is not surprising. Garden deep beds are like the deep beds that are created mechanically in modern potato fields. They are also very like the 'lazy beds' of Ireland and Highland Scotland which evolved to maximize use of available soil, maximize the benefit of seaweed and/or manure and create good drainage in a very wet climate.

Once, while on holiday, I strolled along the machair on the island of Eriskay and came across a crofter harvesting 'Duke of York' and 'Sharpe's Express' from his lazy bed with a tool that looked like a narrow sickle without an edge. The machair is the low ground along the western edge of the Outer Hebrides, made up of wind-blown shell sand and famous for the extraordinary number of wild flowers that grow on it. To make the small lazy beds of the Highlands and Islands, crofters sometimes carried soil in baskets from wherever they could find it to sheltered hollows near the shore. This huge

effort was not necessary in parts of the outer isles – people simply chose a suitable piece of the machair which had not grown potatoes for some time. Using the Celtic foot plough or cascrome (a spade is the more likely tool nowadays), they dug out a rectangular-shaped ditch. The sods lifted first were used (on edge) to create the sides of a lazy bed in the middle of the rectangle. Copious amounts of fresh seaweed were placed in the bed straight on top of the prepared machair surface of the lazy bed and then the seed tubers were placed in a grid pattern equal distances apart on top of the seaweed. The very sandy/shelly soil from the ditch around the bed was then dug out and used to cover the seaweed and potatoes to a depth of several inches. The sickle-like tool, called a crocan, was used to tease out the tubers without digging out large volumes of soil.

The Irish lazy beds were created on a small-field scale using either the Irish version of the foot plough or the long-handled spade/shovel of Ireland. The beds were the length of the field and somewhere between 4ft (1.25m) and 7ft (2m) across. Seaweed and/or manure would be spread in bands on the surface and the potatoes were placed on top; then ditches were created either side by digging out soil and placing it over the top of the bed. The first observers thought this method primitive and lazy because only hand tools were used and a large area of the original surface had only minimum preparation. The English social reformer William Cobbett thought that the potato was 'Ireland's lazy root' and that it encouraged indolence and drunkenness. Any gardener would appreciate the real work involved and the efficient use of time, space and limited resource that the system represents. It also leaves the potato to grow in the greatest depth of soil available with good drainage in a very wet climate. Also, in wet planting conditions, it allows the grower to do as much work as possible with long-handled tools without moving about too much and becoming bogged down in accumulating mud.

Potato barrels are popular. The idea is to start off with a modest amount of potting compost in the bottom of the barrel at planting time and then steadily fill it with more compost as the plants grow. This is supposed to result in layer upon layer of attractive tubers. Potatoes produce an attractive bright skin finish when grown in a peat-based growing medium but most barrels seem to need some modification to prevent compression of the compost under its weight. Growing potatoes need air as well as water and nutrients and most potato barrel crops are disappointing. When the barrel is emptied there is sometimes little but a few distorted tubers and an unpleasant anaerobic smell. Good ventilation, careful watering and some kind of support within the compost should result in better crops.

If garden space is limited, I recommend the use of cheap, black, heavy-duty plastic pots with integral handles. The most common size is about 45cm (18in) across the top. These are sold in garden centres as large plant containers or sometimes water-lily pots. They are big enough to take three or even four seed tubers of a suitable early variety such as the compact 'Swift'. Most potting composts, in reasonable amounts, whether peat-, soil- or organic-alternative-based, suit potatoes. They are disease free, tend to be on the acid side of neutral, hold water evenly and give good skin finish. Regular watering and liquid feeding with a high-potash organic or chemical 'tomato' mix will ensure good crops. The pot can be planted very early, kept outside when conditions allow and moved to a more sheltered position when frost threatens.

PLANTING DISTANCES
Traditional planting distances are:

FIRST AND SECOND EARLIES – 12in (30cm) between tubers in rows 18in (45cm) apart.
EARLY AND LATE MAINCROPS – 15in (37.5cm) between tubers in rows 27in (67.5cm) apart.

WHEN TO PLANT
Planting dates vary greatly from one area to another. When asked about planting times at potato events I usually squirm and too flippantly say, 'Plant one week after your last frost.' In most areas this is sometime in the March–May period. It can be earlier in a few mild coastal areas and I have seen maincrops planted reasonably successfully as late as the third week of June.

I tend to give second earlies more room and early maincrops less room than this. If plants are too close, tuber size is reduced. If plants are too far apart, space is wasted and weeds grow more readily. It pays to get to know the dimensions of your favoured varieties and adjust planting distances so that mature plants touch without being stressed but at the same time maximize weed suppression.

MAINTENANCE

EARTHING UP
When the potatoes have emerged a few inches, earth up the drills with a rake or draw hoe. This gives the plant a volume of soil in which to grow and improves drainage and ventilation around its base. Above all it is a quick, effective way of controlling weeds. Repeat the process as required until the foliage is too big to allow it to happen. In an older age, blacksmith-made ridging tools like mini-double ploughs with a counterweight at the back were pulled through the potato patch to achieve this.

BLIGHT MANAGEMENT
When I first started writing about potatoes the big issue was drought. It seems a long time ago. Now the issues are all to do with excessive wetness – skin finish, internal rust spot and, above all, blight and slugs. First and second earlies are even more popular than they were because they largely avoid these problems if harvested early enough.

Blight is a fungus, *Phytophthora infestans*, which evolved from a seaweed. It needs very high humidity and mild temperatures day and night to grow on potato plants. Initial growth from wind-blown spores is within condensation or rain droplets on the leaves. Current weather patterns suit it well. Until about ten years ago there was only one breeding type of blight in Europe. It produced only asexual spores but still managed to evolve sufficiently to overcome high blight resistance in new varieties within a few years. Now that we have a second breeding type, originally imported in a load of potatoes from Mexico, European blight reproduces sexually and asexually and has even more diversity to help it overcome blight resistance. Current resistant varieties are able to grow for an extra two to four weeks during times of high blight pressure when compared with less resistant varieties. This gives them time to grow a worthwhile crop. It is important that these varieties have good tuber blight resistance – then the spores washed down from the infected foliage into the soil find it difficult to infect the all-important tubers. New varieties are being developed which have blight resistance involving so many genes and mechanisms that resistance lasts longer in terms of both how long it takes to kill off the growing plant and the number of years it takes for virulent blight strains to evolve.

Proprietary fungicides such as Dithane help keep varieties going longer although the preparations available to the gardener are not nearly as effective as the compounds used commercially. Organic growers are still allowed limited use of copper preparations such as Bordeaux mixture. This has the effect of extending the worthwhile growing period, but copper is very toxic and its use is being questioned more and more.

Blight rapidly develops from the droplet infection to form a brown or black circular patch called a lesion. The lesions have a soft, wet appearance and if formed on leaves will show white fungal threads called hyphae on the undersides. In the right conditions these rapidly develop and coalesce. Once more than a third of the foliage is infected it is best to cut and carefully remove the stems and leaves because the tubers will have stopped growing anyway. I use an enclosed compost bin for disposal of this material. Tuber blight infection is reduced if drill surfaces are smooth and free of cracks. Many spores will be washed safely out of the way to the bottom of the drill.

SLUG MANAGEMENT

Population numbers of the underground keeled slugs have exploded in recent years. They are molluscs and thrive in wet conditions. These horrors are the main cause of the dreaded holes in tubers, although wireworm, the misnamed larvae of click beetles, make the very straight holes found in potatoes grown in former grassland or close to grass edges. All varieties can be damaged by slugs, although 'Marfona' and 'Maris Piper' are their favourites. Resistant varieties make a noticeable difference but are not immune. Slug treatments have only a small impact because the main pest species lives underground. Biological controls are becoming more available but their effectiveness depends on perfect timing and getting the solution to where the slugs are developing in soil with an enormous surface area. Harvesting as quickly as possible is important because peak slug damage occurs when the population numbers build up in late summer and autumn.

For details of other potato diseases see pages 29–37.

HARVESTING

First earlies should be harvested fresh as required. If the variety flowers, the opening of the first flower is the sign that there are edible tubers underneath. If your chosen variety doesn't flower, carefully feel about in the drill for signs of small tubers approximately eight to ten weeks after emergence. Many of the low dry matter earlies are best eaten fresh, small and with loose skin. While I admit that there are several exceptions, most earlies have poor dormancy and lose eating quality when stored. I feel that in general the amount planted should be limited to the number that can be used in this way.

Second earlies are often a good compromise. They can be used fresh like first earlies in midsummer or they can be used as set-skin maincrops later. With lots of exceptions, dormancy is on average a little better than is the case of first earlies and eating quality after storage is on average more acceptable.

At the end of the summer or into autumn, whatever type is left (presumably second early, early maincrop or late maincrop) needs to be harvested with storage in mind. After foliage has died back or been cut and removed, tubers need to be left in the ground for two weeks to allow skin set to develop.

Set skin helps stop tubers drying out and becoming rubbery. You can test for skin set by applying firm thumb pressure on the tuber surface. Once the skin has set, the tubers should be harvested immediately and left on the surface for a few hours until dry. Pick out damaged tubers for immediate use. Store the best intact tubers. Potatoes left too long in the ground are susceptible to blight, slugs, soft rots and frosting.

STORAGE

The ideal store area is frost free but cool (c.4ºC/37ºF) and dark with low to medium humidity. Paper and hessian sacks will protect from about one degree of frost but they should be checked for their ability to keep out light. Potatoes exposed to light turn green and are bitter and poisonous because of the glycoalkaloids that build up. Their build-up also occurs during other physiological processes and no bitter potatoes should be eaten even if not green. Potatoes stored in outbuildings must be insulated and kept dark.

Old-fashioned clamps are easy to construct. Pile the potatoes up in a rounded heap on the surface of the cleared potato patch. Cover with a thick layer of straw or similar insulation. Pile as much earth – taken from around the clamp to form a drainage ditch – over the straw as gravity allows, leaving a chimney of straw at the top, through the soil, to allow a little ventilation. Pat the soil firm with the back of the spade. Skin finish does suffer in a clamp because silver scurf fungus flourishes. It is inevitable that the need for extracting potatoes will coincide with the hardest frost of the winter when the clamp surface will be like concrete.

Second earlies and maincrops with poor dormancy should be used first.

FLAVOUR AND STORAGE
Rather like parsnips in winter, cool-stored potatoes sweeten because a little starch turns the sugar to act like very weak anti-freeze. A few days at room temperature before use helps to 'recondition' them. Other more acceptable flavours also develop in storage and some varieties such as 'Golden Wonder' are only at their best after a period of storage.

Potatoes are also liable to pick up unpleasant flavour overtones if stored next to volatile chemicals.

SECOND CROPPING

This has gained in popularity in recent years, particularly in the south of the UK where hard frosts are rare before the year end. Cool-stored first or second early varieties are planted in midsummer to produce a crop of fresh, loose-skin new potatoes as close to Christmas as possible. Firm, waxy varieties which produce salad/small boiling potatoes are favoured, particularly if they store well. Several varieties have been tried but 'Maris Peer' and 'Carlingford' are the most commonly used. Blight is the main reason for failure and I think the first early 'Orla' should be tried with this in mind. Use the space that was occupied by the already harvested earlies unless spare ground exists. Don't be tempted to compromise your rotation. Cheap plastic pots with integrated handles (see page 26) are ideal for small-scale late planting in compost. They can be moved to a frost-free area when cold weather threatens.

POTATO MICROPLANTS

I am personally responsible for the availability of potato microplants in mail-order catalogues and at potato event outlets in the UK and, of course, I think they are absolutely brilliant. Under current legislation it is not possible to certify potato varieties for sale to the public as seed unless they are on the current National List or the EU Common Catalogue. None of the varieties involved – mainly heritage varieties – is now listed. These varieties are all stored as completely disease-free *in vitro* (in glass) microplants in cool, internally lit incubators. They are derived from cells taken from tuber shoot tips, which are then grown on using nutrient gels. Only material known to be disease free can be used for this process. The licensed laboratory that further propagates them by taking tiny cuttings has special permission to produce them for sale because it is recognized that their completely disease-free status means that they are no threat to the health of field crops. This is the only legal means of buying these varieties to grow in the garden.

The process copies the way in which the very highest-grade seed potatoes are initially produced in the UK. These start as mini-tubers grown from microplants. The microplants are grown on in peat compost blocks and dispatched to customers in protective plastic blister packs in early June.

To obtain the best results, grow microplants on in disease-free compost with a view to growing your own disease-free small 'seed' tubers. The cheapest and easiest way is to use a growbag with three to five plants per bag. The enemy if you grow them in garden soil is potato cyst nematode (PCN) (see below). The plants have no tuber and therefore no energy reserve to withstand an infection. The heritage varieties are all sensitive to PCN. The growing plants should be kept free of aphids because they transmit virus from plant to plant. The simplest way is to cover with fleece. Any large tubers harvested can be eaten. Any over 1in (30mm) could be planted in the garden next season, while the remaining mini-tubers should be planted on in compost.

POTATO DISEASES

For blight and slugs, see page 26–7.

POTATO CYST NEMATODE (PCN)
Species of microscopic eelworm can cause huge damage to many varieties, particularly heritage types and others without resistance or immunity. It should be stressed that these pests are minute and should not be confused with any visible pest such as wireworm. Growing potato plants give off root exudates which 'wake up' and attract any hatching larvae in the nearby soil. These swim through the soil water and enter the developing plants through the root system. They live off the plant. Modern resistant plants are hardly checked by this process, while older varieties can become very stunted and yellow, with greatly reduced yields. It is my experience that a majority of mature vegetable gardens and nearly all mature allotments have this pest present.

The most common species is *Globodera rostochiensis* type Ro1, which has a yellow or golden cyst. Susceptible varieties can be greatly debilitated by infection and allow the females to develop. In summer, the females migrate to the fine roots where their bodies form just visible, tiny cysts full of eggs, about 1mm in diameter. These are released into the soil in large numbers to continue the cycle. They can survive for very many years, particularly in light soils. I came across a field in 1977 which was still positive to an eelworm test although the farmer was sure that the field had not grown potatoes since the Second World War. During the war every available tuber was planted and this essential short-term expediency led to large areas becoming eelworm infected.

Varieties which are classified in this book as resistant to PCN are very useful because they break the cycle. The eelworm 'wake up' and parasitize the plant but these varieties shrug off the effects of the invading microscopic nematodes and cause them to turn into males. Varieties that are classified as partially resistant to PCN give good yields but allow a small number of cysts to form. Nature abhors a vacuum and, as resistant varieties take their toll of the golden eelworm, another species, called *Globodera pallida* type Pa 2/3, is becoming more common in this environmental niche. This has cysts that are white to begin with. In both species the cysts eventually turn brown. There are a small number of varieties with some limited resistance to *G. pallida*. Where PCN-resistant varieties have this resistance as well, I describe them as 'double eelworm resistant'.

BACTERIAL DISEASES
These cause soft rot diseases.

BLACKLEG This is the best known. It is caused by a subspecies of *Erwinia carotovora*. The leg is the underground part of the potato stem. When this is infected, usually from the seed tuber, it turns black and rots. The infection quickly spreads up the stem and to the developing tubers. The whole plant steadily turns yellow and slumps. The spores can be transmitted on seed tubers but they are also commonly found in soil. All varieties are susceptible but the infection is more common on earlies and seems to develop particularly when plants are stressed. Cold, wet conditions usually result in crops having above-average levels. There are varietal differences. 'Record' often gets blackleg in single stems and consequently is always a difficult crop to rogue if blackleg is present. 'Desiree' can get high levels of blackleg in hot, dry conditions.

COMMON SOFT ROTS Other bacterial soft rots are also caused by other species and subspecies of *Erwinia* but these don't have the distinctive black colour. These are often secondary infections after mechanical damage or the activities of other organisms allow entry of the infection.

BROWN ROT AND RING ROT These are two very threatening bacterial diseases endemic in most countries in the world, which spread mainly through infected seed. These are notifiable diseases with similar symptoms, and strong measures are taken to stop infection in seed crops. They have never been found in seed crops in Scotland or Ireland. The preventative measures may lead to some varieties covered in this book being unavailable, or at least less available, in the UK and Ireland. At present these varieties are only available as seed grown in such countries as France, Germany, Denmark and the Netherlands. I hope that this situation will lead to disease-free clones of these varieties being planted in, for example, Scotland to initiate stocks of certified seed guaranteed to be free of these rots. This may be a forlorn hope because some of the varieties have only been registered for Plant Variety Rights in a limited number of countries and the breeder could not collect royalties on UK seed crops. Other varieties are too prone to blackleg in the colder, wetter conditions of Scottish and Irish fields. Some companies are reducing seed growing in Scotland and Ireland simply because yields are lower and transport costs are higher.

Brown rot is caused by a bacterium, *Ralstonia solanacearum*. Infected plants may wilt, grow in a stunted way or become yellow as the vessels which conduct sugar around the plant become infected. Cut tubers are distinctly brown around these vessels which form the vascular ring. These cut cells may even exude strands of bacterial slime. If the infection spreads to the eyes soil sticks to them in a characteristic way. Eventually the whole tuber rots. Brown rot used to be a disease of warmer countries but has been found increasingly in temperate areas including most European countries. It can be spread through rough contact with infected tubers or contaminated surfaces. It can infect several other hosts including many other plants of the *Solanaceae* family. There are worries that infection could be spread through irrigation because infected nightshade species have been found growing close to water courses which may carry the bacterium as a result of run-off from vegetable-washing plants or sewage contamination.

Ring rot is caused by a bacterium, *Clavibacter michiganensis*. Foliar wilt may occur fairly late in the season. Infected cut tubers show discolouration of the vascular ring. If infection is advanced enough, squeezing the tubers causes disgusting, cheesy exudates to appear. Infected tubers will eventually completely rot. Infection is spread by planting seed with slight or dormant infection and by contact with infected tubers or contaminated surfaces. This disease is specific to potatoes. It is a disease of cooler climates and it can stay dormant for long periods.

VIRAL DISEASES

These were the diseases, along with blight, which forced the development of new varieties. They are the main reason gardeners are recommended to purchase clean, certified seed tubers every year rather than replant some of the tubers harvested from last year's garden crop.

SEVERE MOSAIC, caused by virus Y, is spread by aphids. It is called 'severe' because not only does it cause a mottle, but there is usually marked distortion of the leaves in infected plants. The severity of symptoms varies greatly with potato variety, strain of the virus and the number of years the infection has been present. Primary infection can be very light but usually, within a few years, the progeny are severely infected and incapable of producing a worthwhile crop. When the infection is established and the seed tuber is infected, the plant produced is brittle, stunted and mottled. Necrotic areas develop in the leaves. These spread and join up until the whole leaf is dead and hanging by a thread of dead petiole. This is classic 'leaf streak', recognized long ago as a sure sign of 'degeneration'.

As roguers, we used to spend days seeking out a mild form of virus Y with only a light mottle called venal necrosis, which was present in a small number of varieties. The necrosis occurs not in potatoes but in tobacco when infected with this strain of virus. There was a zero tolerance in the seed schedule and this combined with the mildness of symptoms made life difficult. We dreaded the phrase 'passed subject to leaf test being negative for VN' – a leaf extract was tested on tobacco plants in a greenhouse and the test took weeks. Eventually someone noticed that Scotland no longer exported seed potatoes to any country growing tobacco and the whole rigmarole disappeared instantly in a cost-cutting measure. Venal necrosis is now treated like any other strain of virus Y with a very low tolerance rate allowed.

LEAF ROLL, caused by potato leaf roll virus (PLRV), has a broadly similar story to that of severe mosaic. It is spread by aphids, the infection becomes greater with time and there is a severe impact on productivity. Aphid frequency and the prevalence of virus within the population of aphids decreases towards the north of the UK (which is why the best seed in Europe comes from Scotland). Initial infection in the growing tops is difficult to spot – just a few twisted leaves that could as easily be insect damage. The infection in the following year comes from the seed tuber and it takes a little time to express symptoms. The bottom leaves curl inwards, starting from the edge, and the symptoms steadily spread up the plant as it develops. The virus blocks vascular tissue and the rolled leaves are very turgid and 'rattle' if shaken. In following years, as the virus level increases, the symptoms are more extreme and express more quickly, and yield plummets. This was described as the 'curl' form of degeneration in earlier times before the existence of virus was known.

MILD MOSAIC, caused by virus X, is probably the most common viral disease. It is classically described as mottle without distortion of the leaf, although relatively severe forms cause some distortion. The infection is spread by contact, either from plant to plant or when man, machine or animal passes through the crop. The virus can remain alive on damp surfaces for many days. The worst infection I ever came across was in a crop produced from brushed seed where the stiff plastic bristles of the rotating brushes had infected every one of the muddy tubers as they passed through the grading machine before planting. The heaviest infection possible in a susceptible variety will lead to a yield decrease of about 15 per cent. Many of the established varieties are immune to virus X.

OTHER MOSAICS Mild mosaic symptoms can occasionally occur when plants are infected by other viruses such as A, S and M. Unlike virus X, these are carried by aphids. A form of virus M caused para-crinkle in 'King Edward'. From its introduction 'King Edward' was always described as having a wavy leaf edge. When techniques were developed to clear varieties of virus, one strange side effect was that 'King Edward' developed a straight edge for the first time in its existence.

SPRAING This is a condition caused by two viruses. Lines, dots, chevrons or arcs of corky material form within and spoil the tuber flesh. The leaves can have bright yellow markings, with or without leaf distortion. The condition is not often passed on in seed to the next generation. The most common type of spraing virus, called tobacco rattle virus (TRV), is carried in light, sandy soils by a free-living nematode (not the potato-specific cyst nematode). The other type, called mop top virus (MTV), is transmitted by powdery scab fungus in cool, wet conditions. In a few varieties this virus can induce a 'mop' of wavy leaves to grow as a bunch at the top of the plant and this phenomenon is presumably responsible for the descriptive name. Different varieties vary greatly in their susceptibility to both these viruses.

There are other causes of conditions similar to spraing. One of them is internal rust spot, caused by the plant not being able to absorb enough calcium in fast growing conditions. I have a suspicion that some of the TRV-resistant varieties are also less prone to internal rust spot.

DISEASES CAUSED BY FUNGI AND ACTINOMYCETES

Blight and wart disease have already been described (see pages 26 and 19) because of their historically important role in the development of varieties.

COMMON SCAB (*Streptomyces scabies*) is caused by an actinomycete. This is an organism that exhibits some of the characteristics of fungi and some of bacteria. It is carried on tubers but is also very common in soil. Actinomycetes can live in drier and more alkaline conditions than fungi and, indeed, common scab is more obvious in dry and limy conditions. The warty scab-like growths infect only the skin of the tubers and can range in degree from hardly noticeable to horrible 'hedgehogs'. Scab does not affect yield much but it is unattractive and gives baked potato skin a mouldy taste. Peeling removes the problem.

Common scab is alleviated if soil is on the acid side of neutral and if water availability is regular without being excessive. This is particularly true at an early stage when the young plant is initiating tubers. It is the reason potato fields are irrigated even in rain in late spring/early summer.

My village used to have a famous fish-and-chip cart pulled by a horse. The lady who ran the business was well known for seeking out only the scabbiest of 'Redskin' (bred by William Pollock of Forgandenny in 1932) to fry. Yes, they were cheaper but once peeled were as good as any for the purpose and the higher the dry matter in a potato the better it fries – the lady linked scab infection with dryness. Fifty years later the old folk of the village still give her chips legendary status. Nowadays, when most fresh potato sales are as washed prepacks in supermarkets, scab has become a major issue. I'm afraid that sales trial after trial has shown that good appearance is by far the most important aspect in promoting potatoes in the supermarket environment. There is a great deal of variation in scab resistance between one variety and another. Increasingly the favoured modern variety has low dry matter, attractive appearance and high resistance to scab.

POWDERY SCAB (*Spongospora subterranea*) is caused by a fungus and is most common in cool, wet conditions. Like common scab, powdery scab is more pronounced in limy conditions. It has become far more common in the current climate. Infection is carried on tubers but the spores remain in soil for many years. Symptoms are very similar to those of common scab and the two conditions often occur together when growing conditions vary over a season. Powdery scab has more rounded pustules and when these erupt they give off characteristic sporeballs in a fine powder – hence the name. The presence of the little honeycombed sporeball (made of single-celled spores joined together) when the pustules are examined with a magnifying glass is a sure diagnostic test for the condition but it does not preclude the presence of common scab as well.

There is also a 'cankerous' form which occurs in susceptible varieties where the organism induces outgrowths in the tuber. These can be topped with scab which is often a bit slimy. This is very common and I am often approached at potato events by worried gardeners with 'space invader' tubers. They have obtained information from the library or from the Internet and are convinced that they have an infection of wart disease to contend with; the seriousness of this disease and the legal obligation to report it is high on their minds. I have never seen wart disease except for samples preserved in formalin. It is very rare and well controlled. So far anyway, all samples presented by such worried gardeners have been cankerous powdery scab.

Another symptom of powdery scab is the presence of small tumorous growths in the roots. This can also occur in tomatoes. Varieties have varying resistance and the resistance is not related to that of common scab. Growing conditions are important in determining the level of infection. I remember a valuable seed crop of 'Pentland Javelin' (a variety famous for common scab resistance) being infected badly by powdery scab in a very wet year. With great difficulty and at some expense it was graded to the standard, which is a tolerance of 12.5 per cent maximum skin area scab cover, passed inspection and then sent to a farm near Dover – about as far from Fife as you can go on mainland Britain. The load was rejected by the farmer and sent back to Fife at the expense of the seed grower. It was planted the next year on the original farm and, in drier conditions, produced a very clean crop.

BLACK SCURF (*Rhizoctonia solani*) is caused by a very common soil fungus which attacks many crop species, with a variety of symptoms. On potato tubers it typically produces obvious, black, tarry-looking spore bodies which, at an early stage anyway, can be scrubbed off. As with the two forms of scab, this has received more attention with the increasing importance of prepacked washed potatoes. The fungus attacks the leg and roots of the plant and leaves brown cankers around the stem base. There is often a ring of white fungal hyphae around the stem where it leaves the soil and the plant is very stressed with a 'hard', 'choked' appearance. The stems are fewer than normal but thicker and woodier. The colour of the plant is darker with much increased pigmentation and a stronger flower. Leaf veins are deeply indented, there is an increase in secondary growth and sometimes aerial tubers are formed in the axils. There are always debates in seed fields about whether a scatter of aberrant plants are examples of *Rhizoctonia* infection or genetic variations.

SILVER SCURF (*Helminthosporium solani*) is caused by a fungus. It is carried on infected tubers but is very common in soil. It grows best in wet conditions and is greatly stimulated when potatoes with plenty of clinging soil are stored in moist, warm conditions. The fungal hyphae feed from the skin surface and give the potatoes a silvery appearance. On close examination, small, round, black sporing bodies can be made out among the fungal threads. The surface cells die and the skin is left bronzed or even cracked and shrivelled. With heavy all-over infection it can be impossible to tell the colour of the skin. Infected tubers dehydrate and become rubbery. Grading to remove excess soil and infected tubers followed by storage at low temperature prevents spread. This scurf can be a problem commercially where appearance is all and it is also very common on garden stored tubers.

BLACK DOT (*Colletotrichum atramentarium*) This is a bit like a dry-weather version of silver scurf. It was once thought to be quite rare and of no economic importance. The demands of supermarket packers for perfect visual appearance have led to it being noticed and highlighted as a significant problem. It can cause wilting in already mature plants and, on tubers, creates very similar symptoms to those of silver scurf. The black sporing bodies (sclerotia) which give it its common name have a different appearance from those of silver scurf when the two are compared under a lens. Those of black dot have a covering of hair-like growths.

GANGRENE (*Phoma exigua* spp.) is the result of a fungus that causes very distinctive rots in stored potatoes, particularly in cold conditions. Small areas of damage become infected and black 'thumbprint' impressions develop. These can be quite small and look fairly innocuous but are a problem for growers because infected tubers never seem to produce healthy plants. Secondary infections of *Erwinia* and other soft rots may be present when whole tubers rot after an initial gangrene infection. Experienced growers of varieties prone to gangrene are even more careful than usual to avoid mechanical damage during harvesting. They are also very keen to develop complete skin set before lifting and to allow just-harvested tubers to 'cure' – that is, to heal small wounds in fairly warm, humid conditions. In gangrene the boundary between infected and uninfected tissue is distinct, mould is white or yellow and the spore bodies are black.

DRY ROT (*Fusarium* spp.) is a fungal disease which can superficially resemble gangrene. It is a rot disease of stored potatoes, particularly in relatively warm conditions. It forms black depressions, often with the surface wrinkled into a concentric ring pattern. Mould is white, pink or blue in appearance. There is not a clear boundary between infected and uninfected tissue. Varieties vary in their resistance to the condition.

SKINSPOT (*Polyscytalum pustulans*) is a fungal disease which attacks all underground parts of the plant but is best known for causing pimple-like growths on tuber skin. It has economic importance when it infects, for example, 'King Edward' because it causes extensive bud damage which results in blanks and poorly growing plants. The pimples are surrounded by a dark sunken ring and are often mistaken for powdery scab pustules. Skinspot often develops in tubers stored in cold, unventilated conditions, particularly after a wet harvest. Varieties vary in their general resistance, and resistance to bud damage is the most important aspect to be considered.

TARGET SPOT OR EARLY BLIGHT (*Alternaria solani*) is a common fungal disease of little or no economic importance. I get the impression that the 'early blight' common name gives it more prominence than it deserves. Round black 'targets' develop in warm, dry weather, particularly on senescing leaves. These can coalesce to form dry necrotic patches but, compared with real blight, progress is slow, the appearance is much drier and no white hyphae are obvious on the underside of the spots. In some earlies such as 'Swift' the presence of *Alternaria* is almost a symptom of senescence.

WATERY WOUND ROT (*Pythium ultimum*) This is a fungal disease which develops at the start of storage. As the name implies, it is a disease of damaged areas of potatoes. The spores are picked up from the soil during harvesting. It is found in most growing seasons but is only extensive when potatoes are harvested roughly and in a somewhat premature state during warm weather. Infection spreads from the point of damage and a very wet, pulpy area develops within the potato. The infected area turns black and cavities form. Secondary infections involving other organisms usually follow and eventually only unpleasant wetness is left.

PINK ROT (*Phytophthora erythroseptica*) is a fungal disease which is occasionally important when a crop is grown in soil with a history of potato growing, the summer is hot and dry and yet the soil is wet. It is most likely in established ware-growing areas under irrigation. Plant roots and stem bases may become infected, causing some wilting, which may not be noticed. It is at this stage that thick-walled resting spores are formed which can eventually find their way into the soil. These can infect the tubers of subsequent crops. The infection usually starts from the stolon (heel) end of the tuber. Liquid leaks from the tubers and soil adheres to them in a characteristic way. The tubers are moderately firm but, when cut open, the infected area goes through a distinctive colour change and gives off a vinegary smell. After a few minutes the cut tuber turns pink; it darkens with time and eventually becomes almost black. There is a clear boundary between infected and uninfected areas.

VIOLET ROOT ROT (*Helicobasidium purpureum*) is a fungal disease which only rarely attacks potatoes. I had considered omitting it but the recent occurrence of one infected tuber in my own garden made me change my mind. I found the appearance disconcerting and it made me realize that it would be one of the conditions that would have readers rushing to their guides. The skin of an infected tuber is covered in an open mesh of obvious strands of purple or brownish-purple fungal growth, and the flesh of infected areas rots and turns brown. The fungus is most commonly found on ground which has been used extensively for growing carrots.

STALK BREAK (*Sclerotinia sclerotiorum*) is a fungal infection which is occasionally common in a localized area of fields and gardens. It is particularly common in oil seed rape and infects subsequent potato crops near by. It causes lettuce drop. It is more common in wet conditions – it used to be said that it was only found in potatoes in the west of Ireland. The fungus attacks a localized area around the stem above ground. The stem usually breaks at this point when the wind catches it. There is a dense mat of white fungal hyphae around and within the stem. A large, black spore body called a sclerotium forms within the centre of the stem like a miniature egg in a nest of cotton wool.

VERTICILLIUM WILT (*Verticillium* spp.) Nearly all garden crops can be infected by a verticillium wilt in hot, dry conditions and potatoes are no exception. *Verticillium* attacks the vascular tissue. The problem is that there can be many other reasons for wilts including various *Erwinia* infections, *Rhizoctonia* and pink rot.

GREY MOULD (*Botrytis cinerea*) All crops can be infected by *Botrytis* and again potatoes are no exception. It is of no economic consequence. It will infect senescing foliage in wet, poorly ventilated conditions. The dying tissue can be covered in the thick grey mould which gives off clouds of spores when disturbed.

PHYSIOLOGICAL DISORDERS

Drought, waterlogging, insect damage, wind damage and even thistle prickling can cause foliar damage. I am going to limit this section to some of the conditions which spoil tubers and don't involve disease organisms.

INTERNAL RUST SPOT, INTERNAL BROWNING AND HOLLOW HEART These are thought to be related conditions caused by a physiological disorder. The latest theory is that insufficient calcium is available for the complete formation of normal tissue. Calcium is a common element but it is not very soluble. In wet, warm conditions the main packing cells of the central part of the tuber (the pith, made of parenchyma cells) are very large and thin walled. These are 'stuck' together with calcium pectate. It seems that, in some varieties, not enough calcium is carried through the plant in the transpiration stream of water and small areas of the tuber flesh break down, die and form brown spots. In some varieties with largish tubers a similar situation causes a brown area to form in the centre, the area furthest away from the source of calcium in the vascular tissue. If the tuber grows even larger, hollow heart develops with a characteristic lining of brown dead tissue.

GROWTH CRACKS These usually occur in medium to large tubers when it rains after a dry spell. The cracks soon 'heal' and a skin forms over the surface of the break. They are of little consequence to the gardener. The odd severe case will make the tuber very difficult to peel. In modern vegetable prepacking factories growth cracks are completely unacceptable and their presence in any numbers leads to rejection. Carefully managed irrigation is used to prevent or lessen the condition.

SECONDARY GROWTH This happens when good growing conditions suddenly occur following a period of poor conditions. The potato grows by producing outgrowths from the main tuber body which has started to 'set' its shape. This can be a simple extension at the stolon (heel) end or it can consist of multiple healthy protruberances combined with growth cracks. In some varieties it can result in 'chain tuberization' where a string of small tubers are formed on the same stolon. In the garden it makes life a little more interesting at harvest time – tubers with secondary growth provide an excuse for playing spot the 'rudest' tuber. At worst, peeling has an element of challenge. Commercially of course it is unacceptable and provides yet another reason for careful management of irrigation on our increasingly industrialized farms.

JELLY END ROT This is not a rot, at least not at the start of the process. It occurs at the stolon (heel) end of the tuber. If the cells here are lacking in starch they are soft and translucent and break down to form an incomplete wet end, which can then begin to rot when secondary infections set in. I have seen this often in 'Pink Fir Apple', a very late variety, when it has not had a long enough growing season to completely fill out the tubers with starch. A good tip is to plant your late maincrops with your first earlies to give them as long a growing season as possible. This is the opposite advice from the standard wisdom of most gardening books. Under certain conditions some varieties exhibit jelly end rot after laid-down starch is turned back into soluble sugar and translocated to other parts of the still growing plant.

LITTLE POTATO This happens to many varieties when the tubers have been kept in store for a long period and have developed long shoots which are unable to reach light. The tubers switch their energy from the production of shoot tissue to small tuber development. Some varieties exhibit little potato if they are planted in a sprouted condition into cold, wet ground. The variety 'Pentland Dell' is particularly prone. When this happens there are an unusual number of blanks in the drill. There are also some initially poor plants which start to produce little potatoes before conditions improve enough to stimulate something approaching normal growth response. A wily Welsh gardener once gave me the tip that you should never plant a tuber in soil that is not warm enough to comfortably push your hand into.

It is just about possible that little potato played a role in bringing potatoes to Europe – see page 9.

FROSTING Most gardeners will already be familiar with this condition. Freezing destroys living potato tissue. Ice crystals expand and cause cells to break down. Symptoms vary with amount of exposure. Affected tubers often 'sweat' on thawing – that is, they become covered in a very obvious sheen of water. Tubers can break down completely, partially or not at all. When cut, fairly solid tubers are usually found to be discoloured inside with brown, grey or black areas. A very characteristic smell develops. When seed which is being chitted is exposed to frost, it is best to be suspicious of any apparently unaffected tubers. Continue chitting and only plant seed with well-developed, healthy shoots. Over-chilled seed is notorious for producing blanks and poorly growing plants.

LENTICEL CONDITIONS The lenticels are the breathing pores on the surface of a stem. Potatoes are modified underground stems and are indeed covered in these small pores. Exhibition varieties tend to have less obvious lenticels.
ENLARGED LENTICELS are found occasionally on tubers growing in water logged conditions, struggling to gain enough oxygen. The enlargement can be quite dramatic and may even cause an eruption of soft tissue. This is readily brushed off.
PIT ROT After wet growing seasons potatoes in store can occasionally develop this condition. Many of the lenticels become surrounded by small black depressions. The condition does not spread and is of little or no concern to most gardeners even if it is noticed. Yet again, it is a condition that adds to the number of sleepless nights suffered by those growing for supermarkets. They, or at least the packers acting on their behalf, find these minor blemishes totally unacceptable.

GUIDE TO POTATO VARIETIES

A NOTE ON THE GUIDE

Each variety name is followed by the date when it was bred, the category of tuber (for an explanation of the categories, see page 22) and the country of origin.

For flavour and the suitability of varieties to different cooking methods, see the note on dry matter opposite.

The ratings are based on National Institute of Agricultural Botany (NIAB) figures where possible. These are independent but not free from controversy. Many maintainers find fault with the procedures involved, and variables such as soil, weather, crop maturity and thickness of skin set can all cause result differences.

TUBER		RESISTANCE	
Yield	1 = very low 9 = very high	Foliage and tuber blight	1 = very susceptible 9 = very resistant
Tuber shape	1 = round 3 = short oval, 5 = oval 7 = long oval, 9 = long	Blackleg	1 = very susceptible 9 = very resistant
Eye depth	1 = very deep 9 = very shallow	Common scab	1 = very susceptible 9 = very resistant
Skin colour	w = white, y = yellow r = red, p = pink b = blue, ru = russet	Powdery scab	1 = very susceptible 9 = very resistant
		Spraing	1 = very susceptible 9 = very resistant
Flesh colour	1 = white, 3 = cream 5 = light yellow 7 = mid-yellow 9 = deep yellow	Potato cyst nematode	s = susceptible r = resistant pr = partially resistant
Dry matter	1 = very low 9 = very high	Slug	1 = very susceptible 6 = highest resistance known
Discolouration	1 = very susceptible 9 = very resistant		
Disintegration	1 = very susceptible 9 = very resistant	Most assessments are based on a scale, usually 1–9: [ ] = my estimate, based on opinion and sources available - = no results available	

YIELD figures are based on a number of field crops and measure marketable harvest before storage. Figures for older varieties are probably underestimates because they are from a time when growing techniques were less sophisticated. The dry matter figure should always be looked at in conjunction with yield. The highest-yielding varieties tend to have low dry matter and achieve some of their bulk from having high water content. Modern varieties also tend to have good appearance, disease resistance and uniformity of size, which leads to higher saleable yields, with fewer outgrades.

TUBER SHAPE can vary depending on the maturity, soil type and growing conditions.

EYE DEPTH is fairly consistent but tuber size can make a difference with some varieties.

SKIN COLOUR can be obscured by green or brown colouring caused by exposure to light. Part-coloured variety patterns and depth of colour can vary a great deal. Skin colour intensity seems to depend on soil type, nutrient availability and growing conditions.

FLESH COLOUR can vary with maturity, nutrient supply, growing conditions and storage time.

DRY MATTER is the non-water content of the potato, much of it being starch. Starch absorbs water and swells as it cooks. Boiling potatoes that don't disintegrate tend to have low dry matter. Frying, crisping and roasting potatoes which don't absorb so much fat and crisp up tend to have high dry matter. High dry matter potatoes also tend to have strong potato flavours which many, including myself, look for. Others dismiss these as being 'earthy'. I find that low dry matter potatoes tend to be 'bland' or 'mild'. Others find these 'fresh' or 'light'. The traditional salad potatoes combine low dry matter and good boiling qualities with good strong flavours. A fine-grained texture also helps make potatoes palatable. Wet, crunchy potatoes are generally less pleasant. Dry matter content and texture vary with growing conditions.

DISCOLOURATION, or after cooking blackening, is harmless but unattractive. All varieties have their inherent disposition but the problem is greatly increased with use of high levels of nitrogen fertilizer.

DISINTEGRATION on boiling is closely related to dry matter content. (There is also a less direct relationship with protein content and cell size.) If high dry matter texture and flavour is preferred, steaming is more successful than direct boiling.

BLIGHT Nowadays blight pressure is greater and blight strains are more variable, and even the most blight-resistant variety can become susceptible. Blight resistance assessments need to be updated frequently. Old figures can be misleading.

BLACKLEG See page 30.

COMMON SCAB See page 32.

POWDERY SCAB See page 33.

SPRAING See page 32. The figures here are for tobacco rattle virus, the most common cause in England and Wales.

POTATO CYST NEMATODE (PCN) OR EELWORM See page 29. The assessments relate to *Globodera rostochiensis*, type Ro1. Where PCN-resistant varieties have resistance to the increasingly common *G. pallida*, type Pa 2/3, I describe them as 'double eelworm resistant' in the text.

SLUG RESISTANCE is of increasing interest. On the 1–9 scale the best available at present is 6. See also page 27.

ACCENT
1989
First early
NETHERLANDS

This is a popular, high-yielding, yellow, ultra-early variety. It produces numerous, uniform, medium-sized, pretty potatoes. Foliar blight resistance is moderately good while tuber blight resistance is fairly poor. It has a word-of-mouth reputation among gardeners for slug resistance.

TUBER		RESISTANCE	
YIELD	8	FOLIAR BLIGHT	5
TUBER SHAPE	4	TUBER BLIGHT	2
EYE DEPTH	5	BLACKLEG	2
SKIN COLOUR	y	COMMON SCAB	7
FLESH COLOUR	5	POWDERY SCAB	6
DRY MATTER	4	SPRAING	8
RESISTANCE TO DISCOLOURING	6	POTATO CYST NEMATODE	r
RESISTANCE TO DISINTEGRATION	6	SLUG	-

ACCORD
1996
First early
NETHERLANDS

'Accord' is fairly high yielding, disease resistant and general purpose. It is double eelworm resistant. Tuber blight resistance is higher than foliar. On paper this is a useful variety for the gardener but it is very difficult to find. Some seed is grown in Scotland, which suggests that it is not particularly prone to the soft rots that preclude other earlies from the Continent being grown in the wetter, colder climate of the north.

TUBER		RESISTANCE	
YIELD	7	FOLIAR BLIGHT	3
TUBER SHAPE	5	TUBER BLIGHT	5
EYE DEPTH	6	BLACKLEG	-
SKIN COLOUR	w	COMMON SCAB	6
FLESH COLOUR	3	POWDERY SCAB	7
DRY MATTER	5	SPRAING	8
RESISTANCE TO DISCOLOURING	-	POTATO CYST NEMATODE	r
RESISTANCE TO DISINTEGRATION	-	SLUG	-

ADMIRAL

1998
Early maincrop
UK

This variety produces lots of large, waxy tubers which store well. It has excellent garden disease resistance. It was fairly well received when it was introduced by one of the major catalogues. It has almost gone out of production, however, because of very high field crop outgrades – mainly growth cracks. A tiny amount is being grown for organic production because of its blight resistance.

TUBER		RESISTANCE	
YIELD	[8]	FOLIAR BLIGHT	7
TUBER SHAPE	6	TUBER BLIGHT	6
EYE DEPTH	6	BLACKLEG	4
SKIN COLOUR	w	COMMON SCAB	8
FLESH COLOUR	4	POWDERY SCAB	6
DRY MATTER	[1]	SPRAING	5
RESISTANCE TO DISCOLOURING	[8]	POTATO CYST NEMATODE	r
RESISTANCE TO DISINTEGRATION	-	SLUG	2

AILSA

1984
Early maincrop
SCOTLAND

'Ailsa' is a medium-sized, high-yielding, general-purpose potato bred by the Scottish Crop Research Institute. Typically, it has very good flavour, creamy flesh and a fairly attractive skin. It can do well in a wide range of growing conditions but has a few weaknesses as far as disease resistance is concerned. Grading squads like to take this one home as a 'boiling'.

TUBER		RESISTANCE	
YIELD	8	FOLIAR BLIGHT	4
TUBER SHAPE	3	TUBER BLIGHT	4
EYE DEPTH	8	BLACKLEG	7
SKIN COLOUR	w	COMMON SCAB	4
FLESH COLOUR	3	POWDERY SCAB	3
DRY MATTER	7	SPRAING	3
RESISTANCE TO DISCOLOURING	5	POTATO CYST NEMATODE	s
RESISTANCE TO DISINTEGRATION	5	SLUG	5

AMANDINE
1990s
First early
FRANCE

This is the first early to be marketed as a salad/baker. Presumably when small they are marketed as salads and when large they are promoted as waxy bakers in the 'Marfona' mould. It recently gained a Royal Horticultural Society award for salad use potatoes. It is as pretty and bright as any 'Mariana' × 'Charlotte' selection could be. The tubers grow uniformly.

TUBER		RESISTANCE	
YIELD	[7]	FOLIAR BLIGHT	[4]
TUBER SHAPE	[7]	TUBER BLIGHT	[4]
EYE DEPTH	[7]	BLACKLEG	-
SKIN COLOUR	y	COMMON SCAB	[8]
FLESH COLOUR	[6]	POWDERY SCAB	[5]
DRY MATTER	[3]	SPRAING	-
RESISTANCE TO DISCOLOURING	[7]	POTATO CYST NEMATODE	s
RESISTANCE TO DISINTEGRATION	[7]	SLUG	-

AMBO
1996
Early maincrop
IRELAND

'Ambo' is a fairly high-yielding, general-purpose TEAGASC variety selected from a 'Cara' × 'Desiree' cross. It has spectacularly attractive, part-red, large tubers. It gains reasonable blight resistance from the 'Cara' side but misses out on eelworm resistance.

TUBER		RESISTANCE	
YIELD	7	FOLIAR BLIGHT	6
TUBER SHAPE	6	TUBER BLIGHT	5
EYE DEPTH	5	BLACKLEG	4
SKIN COLOUR	w/r	COMMON SCAB	5
FLESH COLOUR	3	POWDERY SCAB	3
DRY MATTER	5	SPRAING	3
RESISTANCE TO DISCOLOURING	5	POTATO CYST NEMATODE	s
RESISTANCE TO DISINTEGRATION	6	SLUG	5

AMINCA
1977
First early
NETHERLANDS

This variety comes and goes and sometimes only low-grade seed is available. It is occasionally found in organic outlets. Its high yields, considerable resistance to spraing and resistance to golden eelworm make it a suitable choice for some problem gardens and allotments.

TUBER		RESISTANCE	
YIELD	8	FOLIAR BLIGHT	2
TUBER SHAPE	5	TUBER BLIGHT	3
EYE DEPTH	5	BLACKLEG	I
SKIN COLOUR	y	COMMON SCAB	5
FLESH COLOUR	4	POWDERY SCAB	-
DRY MATTER	4	SPRAING	9
RESISTANCE TO DISCOLOURING	8	POTATO CYST NEMATODE	r
RESISTANCE TO DISINTEGRATION	8	SLUG	-

AMOROSA
1990s
First early
NETHERLANDS

'Amorosa' is a very early, rosy-red, salad potato, pretty and smooth when small but becoming rather coarser and more multi-purpose as it matures. It has some reasonable disease resistance and is said by its maintainer to have good flavour.

TUBER		RESISTANCE	
YIELD	[8]	FOLIAR BLIGHT	[4]
TUBER SHAPE	[6]	TUBER BLIGHT	[6]
EYE DEPTH	[7]	BLACKLEG	[5]
SKIN COLOUR	r	COMMON SCAB	[6]
FLESH COLOUR	[6]	POWDERY SCAB	[4]
DRY MATTER	[4]	SPRAING	[8]
RESISTANCE TO DISCOLOURING	[6]	POTATO CYST NEMATODE	s
RESISTANCE TO DISINTEGRATION	[6]	SLUG	-

AMOUR
1989
Early maincrop
SCOTLAND

This is a Scottish Crop Research Institute 'Cara' cross selection. Like many of these crosses, it is red eyed, high yielding, waxy and fairly disease resistant. Grown by exhibitors such as world potato champion Peter Clark, it is also very pretty.

TUBER		RESISTANCE	
YIELD	[8]	FOLIAR BLIGHT	5
TUBER SHAPE	5	TUBER BLIGHT	5
EYE DEPTH	7	BLACKLEG	4
SKIN COLOUR	w/r	COMMON SCAB	4
FLESH COLOUR	3	POWDERY SCAB	1
DRY MATTER	1	SPRAING	-
RESISTANCE TO DISCOLOURING	8	POTATO CYST NEMATODE	r
RESISTANCE TO DISINTEGRATION	-	SLUG	-

ANNA
1994
Early maincrop
IRELAND

'Anna' is a TEAGASC variety with large yields of appealing, smooth, uniform, waxy tubers. It has had National Institute of Agricultural Botany (NIAB) provisional recommendation. This is one that has been overlooked by most outlets.

TUBER		RESISTANCE	
YIELD	8	FOLIAR BLIGHT	3
TUBER SHAPE	5	TUBER BLIGHT	4
EYE DEPTH	6	BLACKLEG	4
SKIN COLOUR	w	COMMON SCAB	7
FLESH COLOUR	3	POWDERY SCAB	2
DRY MATTER	3	SPRAING	3
RESISTANCE TO DISCOLOURING	5	POTATO CYST NEMATODE	r
RESISTANCE TO DISINTEGRATION	7	SLUG	4

ANYA
1995
Second early
SCOTLAND

This is an oddity. A Scottish Crop Research Institute 'retro' breeding programme project was commissioned to supply Sainsbury's with an 'old-fashioned' salad which the supermarket packers could control with modern Plant Variety Rights. It is a 'Desiree' × 'Pink Fir Apple' which has lost some of the more undesirable characteristics of 'Pink Fir Apple' but still produces a pleasant, nutty, 'semi'-knobbly salad potato.

TUBER		RESISTANCE	
YIELD	2	FOLIAR BLIGHT	4
TUBER SHAPE	8	TUBER BLIGHT	4
EYE DEPTH	4	BLACKLEG	6
SKIN COLOUR	P	COMMON SCAB	8
FLESH COLOUR	2	POWDERY SCAB	6
DRY MATTER	6	SPRAING	[1]
RESISTANCE TO DISCOLOURING	7	POTATO CYST NEMATODE	S
RESISTANCE TO DISINTEGRATION	7	SLUG	[5]

APPELL
c.2000
Maincrop
NETHERLANDS

This is a very recent variety still being assessed by its maintainer, the Dutch Co-op Agrico – probably the largest potato concern in Europe. Initial assessments suggest it is a waxy maincrop producing medium-sized crops of small/medium waxy tubers which may be suitable for salad use. Results are confusing but it seems to have high blight resistance and it is being grown and sold by Bioselect, the organic arm of Agrico.

TUBER		RESISTANCE	
YIELD	[7]	FOLIAR BLIGHT	[7]
TUBER SHAPE	[5]	TUBER BLIGHT	[8]
EYE DEPTH	[7]	BLACKLEG	-
SKIN COLOUR	w	COMMON SCAB	[5]
FLESH COLOUR	[3]	POWDERY SCAB	-
DRY MATTER	[3]	SPRAING	-
RESISTANCE TO DISCOLOURING	-	POTATO CYST NEMATODE	-
RESISTANCE TO DISINTEGRATION	-	SLUG	-

ARGOS
1994
Early maincrop
SCOTLAND

This is a waxy, very high-yielding variety produced by Scotland's greatest living potato breeder, Jack Dunnett, working in Caithness in the far north of Scotland. It is double eelworm resistant and drought resistant, 'designed' to be grown in hot climates. It can be very wet when grown in the UK, particularly in the north. It is found occasionally at potato events and a few independent outlets.

TUBER		RESISTANCE	
YIELD	[8]	FOLIAR BLIGHT	-
TUBER SHAPE	[5]	TUBER BLIGHT	-
EYE DEPTH	[6]	BLACKLEG	-
SKIN COLOUR	w	COMMON SCAB	-
FLESH COLOUR	[3]	POWDERY SCAB	-
DRY MATTER	[3]	SPRAING	-
RESISTANCE TO DISCOLOURING	-	POTATO CYST NEMATODE	r
RESISTANCE TO DISINTEGRATION	-	SLUG	-

ARRAN BANNER
1927
Early maincrop
SCOTLAND

Donald Mackelvie produced this variety on the Isle of Arran. It was once famous for yield, dependability and tolerance to variable conditions. It was the main 'Cyprus potato' at one time and is still sought after in Northern Ireland. Its flavour and cooking characteristics were always the subject of debate, probably because they vary greatly in different growing conditions.

TUBER		RESISTANCE	
YIELD	6	FOLIAR BLIGHT	5
TUBER SHAPE	I	TUBER BLIGHT	5
EYE DEPTH	4	BLACKLEG	-
SKIN COLOUR	w	COMMON SCAB	4
FLESH COLOUR	I	POWDERY SCAB	-
DRY MATTER	-	SPRAING	4
RESISTANCE TO DISCOLOURING	[3]	POTATO CYST NEMATODE	s
RESISTANCE TO DISINTEGRATION	-	SLUG	-

ARRAN COMET
1957
First early
SCOTLAND

This was Donald Mackelvie's swansong. It was famous in its day for yield (of few but large tubers) and earliness along with disease resistance. It is now surpassed by some modern varieties but by fewer than is generally appreciated and it has flavour, drought resistance and weed-suppressing vigour on its side.

TUBER		RESISTANCE	
YIELD	8	FOLIAR BLIGHT	4
TUBER SHAPE	6	TUBER BLIGHT	4
EYE DEPTH	6	BLACKLEG	4
SKIN COLOUR	w	COMMON SCAB	5
FLESH COLOUR	2	POWDERY SCAB	4
DRY MATTER	5	SPRAING	1
RESISTANCE TO DISCOLOURING	5	POTATO CYST NEMATODE	S
RESISTANCE TO DISINTEGRATION	6	SLUG	-

ARRAN CONSUL
1925
Early maincrop
SCOTLAND

This is another 'Arran' selection by Donald Mackelvie – the best variety ever for storing. The growing of 'Arran Consul' was greatly encouraged during the Second World War as it fed the country from April to June and earned the nickname 'the potato that won the war'. Opinions on flavour and cooking were always varied.

TUBER		RESISTANCE	
YIELD	4	FOLIAR BLIGHT	4
TUBER SHAPE	3	TUBER BLIGHT	6
EYE DEPTH	3	BLACKLEG	-
SKIN COLOUR	w	COMMON SCAB	5
FLESH COLOUR	3	POWDERY SCAB	-
DRY MATTER	-	SPRAING	6
RESISTANCE TO DISCOLOURING	3	POTATO CYST NEMATODE	S
RESISTANCE TO DISINTEGRATION	-	SLUG	-

ARRAN PILOT
1930
First early
SCOTLAND

'Arran Pilot' was Mackelvie's most successful selection. It dominated the early market for thirty years before acreage declined rapidly. It is still the most popular garden variety in the UK. Tubers, even from the same plant, vary greatly in size and shape. It needs the shelter and well-prepared soil of a garden to thrive. The flavour and cooking qualities are best in the middle of the early season.

TUBER			RESISTANCE	
YIELD	6		FOLIAR BLIGHT	4
TUBER SHAPE	5		TUBER BLIGHT	3
EYE DEPTH	[6]		BLACKLEG	-
SKIN COLOUR	w		COMMON SCAB	7
FLESH COLOUR	l		POWDERY SCAB	5
DRY MATTER	5		SPRAING	9
RESISTANCE TO DISCOLOURING	7		POTATO CYST NEMATODE	S
RESISTANCE TO DISINTEGRATION	8		SLUG	-

ARRAN VICTORY
1918
Late maincrop
SCOTLAND

This is the oldest 'Arran' variety still available. It is high yielding, given a long growing season. The vivid blue/purple skin contrasts with the bright white flesh. It is floury, very tasty and makes wonderful mash. The foliage is vigorous and weed suppressing. It was kept going in Northern Ireland and a corner of south-west Scotland until it was picked up in recent times by some of the seed catalogue companies.

TUBER			RESISTANCE	
YIELD	[5]		FOLIAR BLIGHT	[6]
TUBER SHAPE	2		TUBER BLIGHT	[5]
EYE DEPTH	3		BLACKLEG	-
SKIN COLOUR	b		COMMON SCAB	[5]
FLESH COLOUR	l		POWDERY SCAB	-
DRY MATTER	[8]		SPRAING	-
RESISTANCE TO DISCOLOURING	-		POTATO CYST NEMATODE	S
RESISTANCE TO DISINTEGRATION	-		SLUG	-

ATLANTIC
1990
Early maincrop
USA

This is a high dry matter variety grown commercially in Europe because, when processed, it produces the pale crisps that are now popular. It is also PCN (eelworm) resistant. Like many processing varieties it has good flavour.

TUBER		RESISTANCE	
YIELD	5	FOLIAR BLIGHT	3
TUBER SHAPE	4	TUBER BLIGHT	3
EYE DEPTH	5	BLACKLEG	5
SKIN COLOUR	y	COMMON SCAB	6
FLESH COLOUR	3	POWDERY SCAB	-
DRY MATTER	8	SPRAING	l
RESISTANCE TO DISCOLOURING	6	POTATO CYST NEMATODE	r
RESISTANCE TO DISINTEGRATION	4	SLUG	5

AVALANCHE
1989
Early maincrop
NORTHERN IRELAND

This is a rarity in every sense. It is a fairly modern variety with high yields of attractive, low dry matter tubers, yet it has very good flavour. It makes a very fine light mash. Only small amounts are grown and its lack of significant disease resistance probably will not encourage greater commercial production in the future.

TUBER		RESISTANCE	
YIELD	7	FOLIAR BLIGHT	4
TUBER SHAPE	4	TUBER BLIGHT	3
EYE DEPTH	7	BLACKLEG	2
SKIN COLOUR	w	COMMON SCAB	5
FLESH COLOUR	3	POWDERY SCAB	3
DRY MATTER	3	SPRAING	l
RESISTANCE TO DISCOLOURING	7	POTATO CYST NEMATODE	s
RESISTANCE TO DISINTEGRATION	5	SLUG	3

AVONDALE
1982
Late maincrop
IRELAND

This is an all-white 'Cara' sport which sometimes reverts to light 'Cara' colouring.

TUBER		RESISTANCE	
YIELD	8	FOLIAR BLIGHT	6
TUBER SHAPE	3	TUBER BLIGHT	7
EYE DEPTH	6	BLACKLEG	4
SKIN COLOUR	w	COMMON SCAB	6
FLESH COLOUR	3	POWDERY SCAB	3
DRY MATTER	3	SPRAING	3
RESISTANCE TO DISCOLOURING	7	POTATO CYST NEMATODE	r
RESISTANCE TO DISINTEGRATION	7	SLUG	4

BALLYDOON
1931
First early
SCOTLAND

'Ballydoon' is one of the 'Doon' series bred by John Watson, the plant breeder of McGill & Smith of Ayr. It was never a great commercial success but was prized by enthusiasts because of its flavour and cooking characteristics. In parts of Ireland it is said to be the boiled potato to go with traditional boiled bacon and spring cabbage.

TUBER		RESISTANCE	
YIELD	[5]	FOLIAR BLIGHT	-
TUBER SHAPE	[3]	TUBER BLIGHT	-
EYE DEPTH	[5]	BLACKLEG	-
SKIN COLOUR	w	COMMON SCAB	-
FLESH COLOUR	[2]	POWDERY SCAB	-
DRY MATTER	-	SPRAING	-
RESISTANCE TO DISCOLOURING	[7]	POTATO CYST NEMATODE	S
RESISTANCE TO DISINTEGRATION	[7]	SLUG	-

BALMORAL
1991
Second early
IRELAND

This is an attractive, red-eyed, TEAGASC exhibition type. It has good yields with modest disease resistance.

TUBER		RESISTANCE	
YIELD	7	FOLIAR BLIGHT	3
TUBER SHAPE	6	TUBER BLIGHT	4
EYE DEPTH	5	BLACKLEG	5
SKIN COLOUR	w/r	COMMON SCAB	7
FLESH COLOUR	4	POWDERY SCAB	5
DRY MATTER	4	SPRAING	3
RESISTANCE TO DISCOLOURING	5	POTATO CYST NEMATODE	S
RESISTANCE TO DISINTEGRATION	7	SLUG	4

BARNA
1993
Late maincrop
IRELAND

This is a very high-yielding, attractive, pink-red variety selected from a TEAGASC 'Cara' × 'Desiree' cross. It is a low dry matter, waxy, boiling type. Production is very limited and enthusiasts have had difficulty finding it.

TUBER		RESISTANCE	
YIELD	[9]	FOLIAR BLIGHT	4
TUBER SHAPE	6	TUBER BLIGHT	4
EYE DEPTH	5	BLACKLEG	4
SKIN COLOUR	r	COMMON SCAB	7
FLESH COLOUR	3	POWDERY SCAB	3
DRY MATTER	[2]	SPRAING	6
RESISTANCE TO DISCOLOURING	[7]	POTATO CYST NEMATODE	S
RESISTANCE TO DISINTEGRATION	[6]	SLUG	5

BELLE DE FONTENAY
1885
Early maincrop
FRANCE

This is one of the classic salad potatoes of French cuisine. The tubers are pretty, yellow, smooth, waxy and slightly curved. They can be eaten hot or cold, with or without skin. Flavour improves with storage and is enhanced when cooked with leeks. 'Belle de Fontenay' is often sold as a first early – but it is not. Premature tubers are very bland.

TUBER		RESISTANCE	
YIELD	-	FOLIAR BLIGHT	-
TUBER SHAPE	[7]	TUBER BLIGHT	-
EYE DEPTH	-	BLACKLEG	-
SKIN COLOUR	y	COMMON SCAB	-
FLESH COLOUR	[6]	POWDERY SCAB	-
DRY MATTER	-	SPRAING	-
RESISTANCE TO DISCOLOURING	-	POTATO CYST NEMATODE	S
RESISTANCE TO DISINTEGRATION	[9]	SLUG	-

BF15
1947
Second early
FRANCE

'Belle de Fontenay' is a parent of this variety. The breeder liked the enigmatic trial label and did not bother with a name. This has caused great confusion over the years – every time the variety is rediscovered, potential customers are put off by the 'name'. Currently, worries about GM material being covertly introduced add to the difficulties. However, it is one of the best salad potatoes around and is larger and earlier than its parent.

TUBER		RESISTANCE	
YIELD	-	FOLIAR BLIGHT	-
TUBER SHAPE	[8]	TUBER BLIGHT	-
EYE DEPTH	-	BLACKLEG	-
SKIN COLOUR	y	COMMON SCAB	-
FLESH COLOUR	[6]	POWDERY SCAB	-
DRY MATTER	-	SPRAING	-
RESISTANCE TO DISCOLOURING	-	POTATO CYST NEMATODE	S
RESISTANCE TO DISINTEGRATION	[9]	SLUG	-

BINTJE
1910
Second early/early maincrop
NETHERLANDS

This has the same sort of reputation in the Low Countries and northern France as 'King Edward' has in England. It resists disintegration and is used for all types of cooking. It has a starchy taste and is widely eaten in the form of the frozen chips supplied to catering outlets and supermarkets all over Europe.

TUBER		RESISTANCE	
YIELD	5	FOLIAR BLIGHT	2
TUBER SHAPE	5	TUBER BLIGHT	2
EYE DEPTH	6	BLACKLEG	-
SKIN COLOUR	y	COMMON SCAB	5
FLESH COLOUR	7	POWDERY SCAB	-
DRY MATTER	4	SPRAING	7
RESISTANCE TO DISCOLOURING	8	POTATO CYST NEMATODE	S
RESISTANCE TO DISINTEGRATION	8	SLUG	4

BLANKA
1970
Second early
NETHERLANDS

'Blanka' is an attractive variety which has come and gone regularly over the years. It is a typical Euro spud with high yields and low dry matter. It always looks at its best washed and packed in a plastic bag.

TUBER		RESISTANCE	
YIELD	[8]	FOLIAR BLIGHT	[3]
TUBER SHAPE	[5]	TUBER BLIGHT	[3]
EYE DEPTH	[7]	BLACKLEG	-
SKIN COLOUR	y	COMMON SCAB	[5]
FLESH COLOUR	[4]	POWDERY SCAB	-
DRY MATTER	[3]	SPRAING	-
RESISTANCE TO DISCOLOURING	[5]	POTATO CYST NEMATODE	S
RESISTANCE TO DISINTEGRATION	[7]	SLUG	-

BRITISH QUEEN
1894
Second early
SCOTLAND

This was bred by Archibald Findlay and quickly became the UK's most popular second early. It is rare now in the UK but still dominates summer production in Ireland. Its great flavour and dry, floury texture is legendary. The variety received a Royal Horticultural Society Award of Garden Merit recently – almost exactly 100 years after it and some of its synonyms first did the same thing. Yields are surprisingly high.

TUBER		RESISTANCE	
YIELD	[6]	FOLIAR BLIGHT	-
TUBER SHAPE	3	TUBER BLIGHT	-
EYE DEPTH	7	BLACKLEG	-
SKIN COLOUR	w	COMMON SCAB	-
FLESH COLOUR	l	POWDERY SCAB	-
DRY MATTER	[7]	SPRAING	-
RESISTANCE TO DISCOLOURING	-	POTATO CYST NEMATODE	s
RESISTANCE TO DISINTEGRATION	-	SLUG	-

BUCHAN
1993
Early maincrop
SCOTLAND

This is a Scottish Crop Research Institute variety, with huge yields and some disease resistance, which has failed to gain attention.

TUBER		RESISTANCE	
YIELD	9	FOLIAR BLIGHT	5
TUBER SHAPE	6	TUBER BLIGHT	6
EYE DEPTH	6	BLACKLEG	5
SKIN COLOUR	w	COMMON SCAB	6
FLESH COLOUR	3	POWDERY SCAB	2
DRY MATTER	3	SPRAING	5
RESISTANCE TO DISCOLOURING	5	POTATO CYST NEMATODE	r
RESISTANCE TO DISINTEGRATION	6	SLUG	-

BURREN

1993
Second early/early maincrop
IRELAND

This is a productive, waxy, summer baker produced at TEAGASC by selecting from a 'Spunta' × 'Marfona' cross. It can be very wet if grown in the north of the UK.

TUBER		RESISTANCE	
YIELD	8	FOLIAR BLIGHT	4
TUBER SHAPE	7	TUBER BLIGHT	4
EYE DEPTH	8	BLACKLEG	5
SKIN COLOUR	y	COMMON SCAB	6
FLESH COLOUR	[6]	POWDERY SCAB	5
DRY MATTER	3	SPRAING	-
RESISTANCE TO DISCOLOURING	7	POTATO CYST NEMATODE	S
RESISTANCE TO DISINTEGRATION	-	SLUG	-

CABARET

2001
Second early/early maincrop
UK

This was bred by Cygnet PB, the company that owns what is left of Maris Lane. The breeding is still done in the Cambridge area but much of the trialling and selection is done at the company base in Scotland. 'Cabaret' is an attractive 'Maris Piper' type. It is certainly productive and a little more disease resistant than 'Maris Piper' but its future will depend on how well samples taken from varying sites fry.

TUBER		RESISTANCE	
YIELD	[7]	FOLIAR BLIGHT	3
TUBER SHAPE	7	TUBER BLIGHT	4
EYE DEPTH	6	BLACKLEG	7
SKIN COLOUR	w	COMMON SCAB	4
FLESH COLOUR	3	POWDERY SCAB	5
DRY MATTER	[7]	SPRAING	3
RESISTANCE TO DISCOLOURING	-	POTATO CYST NEMATODE	r
RESISTANCE TO DISINTEGRATION	[5]	SLUG	3

CAESAR
1997
Early maincrop
NETHERLANDS

This is a pretty potato bred from the attractive 'Mona Lisa'. It is aimed at the prepack market. It has long dormancy and therefore stores well.

TUBER			RESISTANCE	
YIELD	7		FOLIAR BLIGHT	5
TUBER SHAPE	7		TUBER BLIGHT	3
EYE DEPTH	7		BLACKLEG	4
SKIN COLOUR	y		COMMON SCAB	5
FLESH COLOUR	5		POWDERY SCAB	7
DRY MATTER	5		SPRAING	7
RESISTANCE TO DISCOLOURING	6		POTATO CYST NEMATODE	r
RESISTANCE TO DISINTEGRATION	5		SLUG	3

CARA
1976
Late maincrop
IRELAND

I am told that this variety was nearly rejected because it is late but it went on to initiate the great reputation of TEAGASC and Ireland as a centre of potato breeding. 'Cara' is the red-eyed tough guy for the garden and allotment. It has high yields, weed-suppressing vigour and high disease resistance. It also looks good and cooks well although the flavour is on the mild side.

TUBER			RESISTANCE	
YIELD	8		FOLIAR BLIGHT	6
TUBER SHAPE	3		TUBER BLIGHT	7
EYE DEPTH	6		BLACKLEG	4
SKIN COLOUR	w/r		COMMON SCAB	6
FLESH COLOUR	3		POWDERY SCAB	3
DRY MATTER	3		SPRAING	3
RESISTANCE TO DISCOLOURING	7		POTATO CYST NEMATODE	r
RESISTANCE TO DISINTEGRATION	7		SLUG	4

CARLINGFORD

1982
Second early
NORTHERN IRELAND

This was produced by the Northern Ireland Plant Breeding Station. It is a 'Maris Peer' boiling/salad type of potato. Like 'Maris Peer', it is often cool stored to be planted very late at home and abroad for second crop 'new' potatoes at the end of the year. These crops need a rigorous blight control regime.

TUBER		RESISTANCE	
YIELD	7	FOLIAR BLIGHT	4
TUBER SHAPE	4	TUBER BLIGHT	2
EYE DEPTH	6	BLACKLEG	4
SKIN COLOUR	w	COMMON SCAB	8
FLESH COLOUR	2	POWDERY SCAB	5
DRY MATTER	3	SPRAING	-
RESISTANCE TO DISCOLOURING	6	POTATO CYST NEMATODE	S
RESISTANCE TO DISINTEGRATION	8	SLUG	4

CATRIONA

1920
Second early
SCOTLAND

This was Archibald Findlay's swansong. 'Catriona' can have beautiful splashes of blue/purple round the eyes and is still used for exhibition purposes. The tubers can be bold, with excellent flavour and cooking characteristics if eaten fresh. Clean ground and good growing conditions are needed to obtain the best results – it does not like any sort of 'check'.

TUBER		RESISTANCE	
YIELD	[5]	FOLIAR BLIGHT	-
TUBER SHAPE	6	TUBER BLIGHT	-
EYE DEPTH	7	BLACKLEG	-
SKIN COLOUR	w/b	COMMON SCAB	-
FLESH COLOUR	5	POWDERY SCAB	-
DRY MATTER	-	SPRAING	-
RESISTANCE TO DISCOLOURING	-	POTATO CYST NEMATODE	S
RESISTANCE TO DISINTEGRATION	-	SLUG	-

CELINE
1999
Second early/early maincrop
SCOTLAND

'Celine' is a fairly new Jack Dunnett variety which is (of course) very pretty. Prominent lenticels often seem to spoil its appearance for exhibition but scab and double eelworm resistance may well make it very suitable for general garden use.

TUBER		RESISTANCE	
YIELD	7	FOLIAR BLIGHT	2
TUBER SHAPE	6	TUBER BLIGHT	4
EYE DEPTH	6	BLACKLEG	4
SKIN COLOUR	r	COMMON SCAB	7
FLESH COLOUR	6	POWDERY SCAB	5
DRY MATTER	[4]	SPRAING	6
RESISTANCE TO DISCOLOURING	6	POTATO CYST NEMATODE	r
RESISTANCE TO DISINTEGRATION	8	SLUG	3

CHARLOTTE
1981
Second early
FRANCE

This is a reliable, high-yielding, waxy, salad type. Good flavour has made it a standard reference variety in the taste tests which are used to judge the flood of new salad varieties. Many of these have 'Charlotte' as a parent yet most are struggling to have anything like the quality. I have been surprised at how large 'Charlotte' can grow in heavy, flinty soils in the south of England.

TUBER		RESISTANCE	
YIELD	7	FOLIAR BLIGHT	2
TUBER SHAPE	7	TUBER BLIGHT	5
EYE DEPTH	6	BLACKLEG	8
SKIN COLOUR	y	COMMON SCAB	4
FLESH COLOUR	6	POWDERY SCAB	4
DRY MATTER	[3]	SPRAING	9
RESISTANCE TO DISCOLOURING	[6]	POTATO CYST NEMATODE	s
RESISTANCE TO DISINTEGRATION	[8]	SLUG	6

CHERIE
1997
Second early
FRANCE

This is a selection from a 'Roseval' cross which also introduced eelworm resistance. It is very pretty and uniform. Unfortunately, I failed to find anything about the flavour to enthuse over. Personal preferences, timing of harvest, texture, amount of sunshine, soil type, rainfall and sometimes length of storage time can greatly influence taste decisions.

TUBER		RESISTANCE	
YIELD	[5]	FOLIAR BLIGHT	-
TUBER SHAPE	[8]	TUBER BLIGHT	[5]
EYE DEPTH	[6]	BLACKLEG	-
SKIN COLOUR	r	COMMON SCAB	[6]
FLESH COLOUR	[5]	POWDERY SCAB	-
DRY MATTER	[3]	SPRAING	-
RESISTANCE TO DISCOLOURING	-	POTATO CYST NEMATODE	r
RESISTANCE TO DISINTEGRATION	[7]	SLUG	-

CLARET
1996
Early maincrop
SCOTLAND

'Claret' is a Scottish Crop Research Institute 'improved' 'Desiree' type. It has a smoother shape and a deeper red skin colour. It also has better common scab and blackleg resistance but it does not have the committed flavour of 'Desiree'. Some would say that this is a good thing. Lack of resistance to eelworm and spraing virus do not help a modern variety to establish itself.

TUBER		RESISTANCE	
YIELD	7	FOLIAR BLIGHT	5
TUBER SHAPE	6	TUBER BLIGHT	6
EYE DEPTH	5	BLACKLEG	5
SKIN COLOUR	r	COMMON SCAB	7
FLESH COLOUR	3	POWDERY SCAB	4
DRY MATTER	5	SPRAING	1
RESISTANCE TO DISCOLOURING	5	POTATO CYST NEMATODE	s
RESISTANCE TO DISINTEGRATION	7	SLUG	2

COLLEEN

1993
First early
IRELAND

This is a TEAGASC variety with similar blight resistance to 'Karlena' and 'Premiere'. It is slightly waxier but commercially it is limited to a small amount of organic production.

TUBER		RESISTANCE	
YIELD	7	FOLIAR BLIGHT	5
TUBER SHAPE	4	TUBER BLIGHT	6
EYE DEPTH	6	BLACKLEG	4
SKIN COLOUR	w	COMMON SCAB	6
FLESH COLOUR	4	POWDERY SCAB	3
DRY MATTER	5	SPRAING	1
RESISTANCE TO DISCOLOURING	6	POTATO CYST NEMATODE	s
RESISTANCE TO DISINTEGRATION	5	SLUG	-

COLMO

1973
First early
NETHERLANDS

This is another Euro variety which has kept going because it has very high yields, waxiness, good appearance and good cooking characteristics in terms of firmness and colour retention.

TUBER		RESISTANCE	
YIELD	8	FOLIAR BLIGHT	2
TUBER SHAPE	5	TUBER BLIGHT	3
EYE DEPTH	6	BLACKLEG	1
SKIN COLOUR	w	COMMON SCAB	4
FLESH COLOUR	5	POWDERY SCAB	-
DRY MATTER	3	SPRAING	3
RESISTANCE TO DISCOLOURING	8	POTATO CYST NEMATODE	s
RESISTANCE TO DISINTEGRATION	8	SLUG	-

CONCORDE

1988
First early
NETHERLANDS

This is a long, very high-yielding, early bulking, yellow, waxy variety. The cooking qualities and eelworm resistance have kept this one going for garden use. It also has a reputation among gardeners for slug resistance.

TUBER		RESISTANCE	
YIELD	9	FOLIAR BLIGHT	4
TUBER SHAPE	7	TUBER BLIGHT	2
EYE DEPTH	6	BLACKLEG	5
SKIN COLOUR	y	COMMON SCAB	6
FLESH COLOUR	7	POWDERY SCAB	-
DRY MATTER	4	SPRAING	1
RESISTANCE TO DISCOLOURING	7	POTATO CYST NEMATODE	r
RESISTANCE TO DISINTEGRATION	8	SLUG	-

COSMOS

1973
Second early
NETHERLANDS

'Estima' is a parent of this high-yielding variety. 'Cosmos' is larger and more blight resistant and has made some impact in organic growing. In the opinion of many commercial growers, there are too many tubers with poor appearance.

TUBER		RESISTANCE	
YIELD	[8]	FOLIAR BLIGHT	6
TUBER SHAPE	6	TUBER BLIGHT	7
EYE DEPTH	5	BLACKLEG	5
SKIN COLOUR	y	COMMON SCAB	7
FLESH COLOUR	5	POWDERY SCAB	4
DRY MATTER	5	SPRAING	-
RESISTANCE TO DISCOLOURING	6	POTATO CYST NEMATODE	s
RESISTANCE TO DISINTEGRATION	5	SLUG	-

CULTRA
1988
Early maincrop
IRELAND

This is a TEAGASC variety with a particularly bright red eye for the 'King Edward' look. It is a general-purpose prepack type with very high yields and good disease resistance, although it may be prone to internal rust spot.

TUBER		RESISTANCE	
YIELD	9	FOLIAR BLIGHT	4
TUBER SHAPE	5	TUBER BLIGHT	5
EYE DEPTH	5	BLACKLEG	6
SKIN COLOUR	w/r	COMMON SCAB	6
FLESH COLOUR	3	POWDERY SCAB	6
DRY MATTER	5	SPRAING	3
RESISTANCE TO DISCOLOURING	6	POTATO CYST NEMATODE	r
RESISTANCE TO DISINTEGRATION	6	SLUG	4

DESIREE
1962
Early maincrop
NETHERLANDS

This is still the world's most popular red. It has enjoyed a comeback in the UK thanks to positive comment from Delia Smith. It is a vigorous, fairly waxy potato with a strong flavour which is at its best when grown in East Anglia. It is very drought resistant but can suffer overwhelmingly from common scab on sandy or gravelly soils.

TUBER		RESISTANCE	
YIELD	7	FOLIAR BLIGHT	4
TUBER SHAPE	7	TUBER BLIGHT	5
EYE DEPTH	5	BLACKLEG	4
SKIN COLOUR	r	COMMON SCAB	4
FLESH COLOUR	5	POWDERY SCAB	7
DRY MATTER	5	SPRAING	3
RESISTANCE TO DISCOLOURING	6	POTATO CYST NEMATODE	s
RESISTANCE TO DISINTEGRATION	7	SLUG	4

DRUID
c.2000
Late maincrop
IRELAND

'Druid' is a vigorous red with all-round disease resistance and good general-purpose cooking qualities. Its late maturity is the most obvious 'problem' at this stage in the information-gathering process.

TUBER		RESISTANCE	
YIELD	[8]	FOLIAR BLIGHT	[6]
TUBER SHAPE	[3]	TUBER BLIGHT	[6]
EYE DEPTH	[7]	BLACKLEG	-
SKIN COLOUR	r	COMMON SCAB	[7]
FLESH COLOUR	[3]	POWDERY SCAB	-
DRY MATTER	[4]	SPRAING	-
RESISTANCE TO DISCOLOURING	[7]	POTATO CYST NEMATODE	r
RESISTANCE TO DISINTEGRATION	[7]	SLUG	-

DUKE OF YORK
1891
First early
SCOTLAND

Bred by William Sim of Fyvie, Aberdeenshire, 'Duke' ('Eersteling' in the Netherlands) quickly gained a reputation for quality which survives to this day. The tubers are pale yellow, smooth and attractive. They are waxy, almost salad potatoes at the start of their season but they quickly mature, dry matter increases and they become very versatile. Despite moans from the 'waxy' brigade about disintegration, they are a flavour reference as far as I am concerned.

TUBER		RESISTANCE	
YIELD	4	FOLIAR BLIGHT	3
TUBER SHAPE	6	TUBER BLIGHT	3
EYE DEPTH	7	BLACKLEG	-
SKIN COLOUR	w	COMMON SCAB	5
FLESH COLOUR	5	POWDERY SCAB	-
DRY MATTER	3-6	SPRAING	6
RESISTANCE TO DISCOLOURING	9	POTATO CYST NEMATODE	s
RESISTANCE TO DISINTEGRATION	9-6	SLUG	-

DUNBAR ROVER
1936
Second early
SCOTLAND

This is an old Celtic fringe favourite bred by Charles Spence of Dunbar. It is one of the best dry, floury varieties in terms of flavour but it is very rare because low yields make it difficult for the grower to make a living. If you like the 'Golden Wonder' or 'British Queen' style of potato, be prepared to pay a premium for 'Dunbar Rover'.

TUBER		RESISTANCE	
YIELD	[3]	FOLIAR BLIGHT	-
TUBER SHAPE	4	TUBER BLIGHT	-
EYE DEPTH	5	BLACKLEG	-
SKIN COLOUR	w	COMMON SCAB	-
FLESH COLOUR	l	POWDERY SCAB	-
DRY MATTER	[8]	SPRAING	-
RESISTANCE TO DISCOLOURING	-	POTATO CYST NEMATODE	S
RESISTANCE TO DISINTEGRATION	-	SLUG	-

DUNBAR STANDARD
1936
Late maincrop
SCOTLAND

This was also bred by Charles Spence of Dunbar. It is very vigorous with huge foliage and large white flowers when grown on eelworm-free ground. In old texts it is recommended for heavy soil. I believe that this was because the foliage was so large that the wind could cause problems if the roots were anchored in very light soil. The tubers have a good strong flavour and have good all-round cooking qualities. They even boil well.

TUBER		RESISTANCE	
YIELD	5	FOLIAR BLIGHT	4
TUBER SHAPE	5	TUBER BLIGHT	4
EYE DEPTH	7	BLACKLEG	-
SKIN COLOUR	w	COMMON SCAB	4
FLESH COLOUR	3	POWDERY SCAB	-
DRY MATTER	5	SPRAING	[3]
RESISTANCE TO DISCOLOURING	5	POTATO CYST NEMATODE	S
RESISTANCE TO DISINTEGRATION	8	SLUG	-

DUNDROD
1987
First early
NORTHERN IRELAND

This was bred by John Clarke of Co. Antrim and released after his death. 'Dundrod' is a typical 'Ulster' in terms of being good as a fresh, first early, boiling potato. It is also general purpose if harvested a little later and is sometimes used for early chip production. It is the only Clarke first early to have eelworm resistance.

TUBER		RESISTANCE	
YIELD	6	FOLIAR BLIGHT	5
TUBER SHAPE	6	TUBER BLIGHT	2
EYE DEPTH	5	BLACKLEG	3
SKIN COLOUR	w	COMMON SCAB	5
FLESH COLOUR	3	POWDERY SCAB	4
DRY MATTER	5	SPRAING	7
RESISTANCE TO DISCOLOURING	7	POTATO CYST NEMATODE	r
RESISTANCE TO DISINTEGRATION	8	SLUG	-

DUNLUCE
1976
First early
NORTHERN IRELAND

This is another John Clarke variety released after the prefix 'Ulster' disappeared. Like all available Clarke first earlies, it is attractive and has the cooking characteristics to be classified as a good, fresh, loose-skin boiling potato.

TUBER		RESISTANCE	
YIELD	6	FOLIAR BLIGHT	2
TUBER SHAPE	2	TUBER BLIGHT	2
EYE DEPTH	7	BLACKLEG	-
SKIN COLOUR	w	COMMON SCAB	4
FLESH COLOUR	1	POWDERY SCAB	6
DRY MATTER	5	SPRAING	4
RESISTANCE TO DISCOLOURING	8	POTATO CYST NEMATODE	s
RESISTANCE TO DISINTEGRATION	8	SLUG	-

EDZELL BLUE

pre-1915
Second early
SCOTLAND

This was first recorded in 1915 but is said to have been bred in Edzell, Angus, in the Victorian era. Its blue skin contrasts with the white, floury flesh. It is dry and tasty, and successful boiling needs experience and care. Cooking 'Edzell Blue's on the farm range was often used as the test for a new cook in East Scotland. Steamers and microwaves make life easier! The variety is very sensitive to eelworm infection.

TUBER		RESISTANCE	
YIELD	-	FOLIAR BLIGHT	-
TUBER SHAPE	2	TUBER BLIGHT	-
EYE DEPTH	3	BLACKLEG	-
SKIN COLOUR	b	COMMON SCAB	-
FLESH COLOUR	l	POWDERY SCAB	-
DRY MATTER	[8]	SPRAING	-
RESISTANCE TO DISCOLOURING	-	POTATO CYST NEMATODE	S
RESISTANCE TO DISINTEGRATION	[1]	SLUG	-

EPICURE

1897
First early
ENGLAND

'Epicure' was bred by James Clark of Christchurch, Hampshire, for Suttons. It is round, deep eyed, floury and tasty. It is famous for recovering quickly from frost damage and has surprisingly high yields. It became the traditional Ayrshire early potato and is still the most popular garden variety in Scotland. The tendency in Ayrshire today to replace it is probably a mistake.

TUBER		RESISTANCE	
YIELD	[8]	FOLIAR BLIGHT	4
TUBER SHAPE	l	TUBER BLIGHT	4
EYE DEPTH	3	BLACKLEG	-
SKIN COLOUR	w	COMMON SCAB	2
FLESH COLOUR	l	POWDERY SCAB	-
DRY MATTER	[7]	SPRAING	-
RESISTANCE TO DISCOLOURING	-	POTATO CYST NEMATODE	S
RESISTANCE TO DISINTEGRATION	[2]	SLUG	-

ERNTESTOLZ
1976
Early maincrop
GERMANY

This is said to have an unusual combination of high dry matter content and resistance to cooking disintegration but relevant figures vary. The variety is certainly used for processing into crisps etc. and is also good for rosti and latkes.

TUBER		RESISTANCE	
YIELD	[7]	FOLIAR BLIGHT	4
TUBER SHAPE	3	TUBER BLIGHT	4
EYE DEPTH	3	BLACKLEG	4
SKIN COLOUR	w	COMMON SCAB	[3]
FLESH COLOUR	5	POWDERY SCAB	-
DRY MATTER	7	SPRAING	-
RESISTANCE TO DISCOLOURING	5	POTATO CYST NEMATODE	S
RESISTANCE TO DISINTEGRATION	5	SLUG	-

ESTIMA
1973
Second early
NETHERLANDS

This helped set the scene for modern Dutch prominence in potato breeding. Along with 'Wilja', it established new standards for yield and uniformity in second earlies. 'Estima' has visual appeal and destroyed the myth that a yellow potato could not be popular in Britain. Opinions on flavour vary widely.

TUBER		RESISTANCE	
YIELD	7	FOLIAR BLIGHT	4
TUBER SHAPE	6	TUBER BLIGHT	5
EYE DEPTH	8	BLACKLEG	2
SKIN COLOUR	y	COMMON SCAB	6
FLESH COLOUR	5	POWDERY SCAB	3
DRY MATTER	4	SPRAING	5
RESISTANCE TO DISCOLOURING	6	POTATO CYST NEMATODE	S
RESISTANCE TO DISINTEGRATION	6	SLUG	4

EXQUISA
1990s
Early maincrop
NETHERLANDS

This is a pretty, yellow, waxy salad/boiler. It is one of a raft of Euro salad potatoes being promoted at the moment. Its long dormancy has led to it being trialled as a second cropper.

TUBER		RESISTANCE	
YIELD	6	FOLIAR BLIGHT	2
TUBER SHAPE	7	TUBER BLIGHT	1
EYE DEPTH	6	BLACKLEG	4
SKIN COLOUR	y	COMMON SCAB	7
FLESH COLOUR	6	POWDERY SCAB	6
DRY MATTER	[4]	SPRAING	7
RESISTANCE TO DISCOLOURING	-	POTATO CYST NEMATODE	r
RESISTANCE TO DISINTEGRATION	-	SLUG	5

FAMBO
1985
Second early
NETHERLANDS

This produces good yields of general-purpose tubers. The disease resistance is not impressive but, with the exception of eelworm, perhaps 'Fambo' has no great susceptibility either.

TUBER		RESISTANCE	
YIELD	7	FOLIAR BLIGHT	4
TUBER SHAPE	7	TUBER BLIGHT	3
EYE DEPTH	7	BLACKLEG	-
SKIN COLOUR	w	COMMON SCAB	5
FLESH COLOUR	4	POWDERY SCAB	-
DRY MATTER	6	SPRAING	7
RESISTANCE TO DISCOLOURING	8	POTATO CYST NEMATODE	s
RESISTANCE TO DISINTEGRATION	5	SLUG	-

FIANNA

1987
Early maincrop
NETHERLANDS

'Fianna' is supposed to be the new 'Maris Piper', with good flavour, high dry matter and good fry colour. It has good dormancy but opinions vary on other storage characteristics. The variety has not taken off as well as was expected.

TUBER		RESISTANCE	
YIELD	[7]	FOLIAR BLIGHT	4
TUBER SHAPE	6	TUBER BLIGHT	3
EYE DEPTH	6	BLACKLEG	6
SKIN COLOUR	y	COMMON SCAB	5
FLESH COLOUR	4	POWDERY SCAB	7
DRY MATTER	9	SPRAING	8
RESISTANCE TO DISCOLOURING	5	POTATO CYST NEMATODE	r
RESISTANCE TO DISINTEGRATION	5	SLUG	4

FOREMOST

1954
First early
UK

This was launched as 'Sutton's Foremost'. From the start it was a gardener's favourite because of its flavour and excellent cooking characteristics. Modern seed production is entirely for garden use.

TUBER		RESISTANCE	
YIELD	5	FOLIAR BLIGHT	4
TUBER SHAPE	4	TUBER BLIGHT	4
EYE DEPTH	[6]	BLACKLEG	-
SKIN COLOUR	w	COMMON SCAB	5
FLESH COLOUR	l	POWDERY SCAB	-
DRY MATTER	5	SPRAING	-
RESISTANCE TO DISCOLOURING	7	POTATO CYST NEMATODE	s
RESISTANCE TO DISINTEGRATION	7	SLUG	-

GOLDEN WONDER
1906
Late maincrop
UK

This is the Scottish russet sport of Clark's English variety 'Maincrop' (or 'Langworthy'). It was found by Mr Brown of Arbroath and is still very highly regarded in Scotland. It is dry, floury and very tasty, particularly if stored until after New Year. It can be extraordinarily dry when grown in the sunnier south. The very best samples are found north of Aberdeen.

TUBER		RESISTANCE	
YIELD	2	FOLIAR BLIGHT	6
TUBER SHAPE	7	TUBER BLIGHT	6
EYE DEPTH	5	BLACKLEG	-
SKIN COLOUR	ru	COMMON SCAB	8
FLESH COLOUR	5	POWDERY SCAB	-
DRY MATTER	9	SPRAING	3
RESISTANCE TO DISCOLOURING	-	POTATO CYST NEMATODE	s
RESISTANCE TO DISINTEGRATION	3	SLUG	[5]

HARMONY
1998
Early maincrop
SCOTLAND

This is a fairly new Jack Dunnett variety which has already had major showbench success. It is a pretty, smooth, waxy white with very high yields. It is partially double eelworm resistant, scab resistant and has the looked-for good firm cooking characteristics.

TUBER		RESISTANCE	
YIELD	[8]	FOLIAR BLIGHT	2
TUBER SHAPE	6	TUBER BLIGHT	3
EYE DEPTH	6	BLACKLEG	2
SKIN COLOUR	w	COMMON SCAB	6
FLESH COLOUR	3	POWDERY SCAB	4
DRY MATTER	3	SPRAING	-
RESISTANCE TO DISCOLOURING	8	POTATO CYST NEMATODE	pr
RESISTANCE TO DISINTEGRATION	6	SLUG	5

HERMES
pre-1994
Early maincrop
AUSTRIA

This is a high dry matter, well-flavoured potato which has replaced 'Record' in the crisp industry. It has the paler fry colour that the industry has decreed to be the modern requirement. As with 'Record', many have found it to be to their taste.

TUBER		RESISTANCE	
YIELD	[7]	FOLIAR BLIGHT	3
TUBER SHAPE	5	TUBER BLIGHT	4
EYE DEPTH	3	BLACKLEG	6
SKIN COLOUR	y	COMMON SCAB	6
FLESH COLOUR	7	POWDERY SCAB	8
DRY MATTER	9	SPRAING	8
RESISTANCE TO DISCOLOURING	2	POTATO CYST NEMATODE	S
RESISTANCE TO DISINTEGRATION	6	SLUG	5

HOME GUARD
1942
First early
SCOTLAND

This was introduced by McGill & Smith of Ayr during the Second World War. Members of the Home Guard helped promote its use, and it quickly became a commercial success because of its early yield. It is still the main early in Ireland and is still popular with gardeners. In my opinion it is an early early which is best eaten early.

TUBER		RESISTANCE	
YIELD	7	FOLIAR BLIGHT	4
TUBER SHAPE	3	TUBER BLIGHT	2
EYE DEPTH	5	BLACKLEG	4
SKIN COLOUR	w	COMMON SCAB	6
FLESH COLOUR	2	POWDERY SCAB	7
DRY MATTER	6	SPRAING	7
RESISTANCE TO DISCOLOURING	2	POTATO CYST NEMATODE	S
RESISTANCE TO DISINTEGRATION	6	SLUG	-

INTERNATIONAL KIDNEY
1879
Early maincrop
ENGLAND

This was bred by Robert Fenn of Sulhamstead, Berkshire. This is the classic old maincrop variety sold early in the season by Jersey growers under the trademark 'Jersey Royal'. If picked prematurely, it is a small, firm, waxy potato. When left to mature naturally, it is a large kidney, floury enough to disintegrate slightly when boiled. Seed catalogues receive complaints about 'phoney' 'Jersey Royal's every summer.

TUBER		RESISTANCE	
YIELD	-	FOLIAR BLIGHT	-
TUBER SHAPE	7	TUBER BLIGHT	-
EYE DEPTH	5	BLACKLEG	-
SKIN COLOUR	y	COMMON SCAB	-
FLESH COLOUR	7	POWDERY SCAB	-
DRY MATTER	-	SPRAING	-
RESISTANCE TO DISCOLOURING	-	POTATO CYST NEMATODE	S
RESISTANCE TO DISINTEGRATION	-	SLUG	-

ISLE OF JURA
c.2000
Early maincrop
UK

This is the latest variety from Cygnet PB using their Cambridge and Scottish facilities. In the company there are family connections with Jura – hence the name. It is a high-yielding, general-purpose white potato aimed at the commercial prepack market. It is at an early stage of development from a company which at least acknowledges that flavour is a factor in variety choice. Apart from blight and slugs, it has some useful resistance to garden problems.

TUBER		RESISTANCE	
YIELD	[8]	FOLIAR BLIGHT	3
TUBER SHAPE	6	TUBER BLIGHT	5
EYE DEPTH	6	BLACKLEG	7
SKIN COLOUR	w	COMMON SCAB	5
FLESH COLOUR	5	POWDERY SCAB	5
DRY MATTER	[5]	SPRAING	7
RESISTANCE TO DISCOLOURING	-	POTATO CYST NEMATODE	r
RESISTANCE TO DISINTEGRATION	-	SLUG	2

JULIETTE
1990s
Early maincrop
FRANCE

This is another of the recent batch of European salads. There is limited reliable trial information available.

TUBER			RESISTANCE	
YIELD	[5]		FOLIAR BLIGHT	[6]
TUBER SHAPE	[7]		TUBER BLIGHT	-
EYE DEPTH	[7]		BLACKLEG	-
SKIN COLOUR	y		COMMON SCAB	-
FLESH COLOUR	[3]		POWDERY SCAB	-
DRY MATTER	[3]		SPRAING	-
RESISTANCE TO DISCOLOURING	-		POTATO CYST NEMATODE	r
RESISTANCE TO DISINTEGRATION	-		SLUG	-

JUNIOR
1991
First early
NETHERLANDS

This is a very early variety which has been repromoted recently by Bioselect, the organic arm of Agrico, presumably because it has high tuber blight resistance. Tuber blight resistance is particularly important in earlies because with resistant varieties once the tubers have formed even serious blight infection has little impact.

TUBER			RESISTANCE	
YIELD	[6]		FOLIAR BLIGHT	[3]
TUBER SHAPE	[3]		TUBER BLIGHT	[7]
EYE DEPTH	[7]		BLACKLEG	-
SKIN COLOUR	y		COMMON SCAB	[6]
FLESH COLOUR	[5]		POWDERY SCAB	-
DRY MATTER	[4]		SPRAING	[7]
RESISTANCE TO DISCOLOURING	[7]		POTATO CYST NEMATODE	r
RESISTANCE TO DISINTEGRATION	-		SLUG	-

KARLENA
1993
First/second early
GERMANY

This is a real find for those who like old-fashioned, floury earlies such as 'Epicure' or 'Sharpe's Express'. It is tasty, versatile and very disease resistant. It will grow well where the old varieties will struggle.

TUBER		RESISTANCE	
YIELD	[7]	FOLIAR BLIGHT	[6]
TUBER SHAPE	[3]	TUBER BLIGHT	[6]
EYE DEPTH	[8]	BLACKLEG	[7]
SKIN COLOUR	y	COMMON SCAB	[7]
FLESH COLOUR	[5]	POWDERY SCAB	-
DRY MATTER	[9]	SPRAING	-
RESISTANCE TO DISCOLOURING	[7]	POTATO CYST NEMATODE	r
RESISTANCE TO DISINTEGRATION	-	SLUG	-

KENNEBEC
1948
Early maincrop
USA

This has been grown in Scotland for seed export for many years. It is a big, tough plant which produces large, firm, creamy tubers which cook well.

TUBER		RESISTANCE	
YIELD	6	FOLIAR BLIGHT	4
TUBER SHAPE	5	TUBER BLIGHT	4
EYE DEPTH	6	BLACKLEG	-
SKIN COLOUR	w	COMMON SCAB	5
FLESH COLOUR	3	POWDERY SCAB	-
DRY MATTER	-	SPRAING	[3]
RESISTANCE TO DISCOLOURING	[7]	POTATO CYST NEMATODE	s
RESISTANCE TO DISINTEGRATION	-	SLUG	-

KERR'S PINK
1917
Late maincrop
SCOTLAND

James Henry of Cornhill, Banffshire, produced this variety from a 'Fortyfold' cross. In the way of the potato world it is now named after a merchant. It is a tall, robust plant which crops well in a long growing season. It is fine grained, floury and very popular in Scotland and Ireland. The potato for a Burns' Night supper.

TUBER		RESISTANCE	
YIELD	5	FOLIAR BLIGHT	6
TUBER SHAPE	3	TUBER BLIGHT	4
EYE DEPTH	5	BLACKLEG	-
SKIN COLOUR	p	COMMON SCAB	4
FLESH COLOUR	3	POWDERY SCAB	-
DRY MATTER	6	SPRAING	5
RESISTANCE TO DISCOLOURING	5	POTATO CYST NEMATODE	s
RESISTANCE TO DISINTEGRATION	5	SLUG	l

KESTREL
1992
Second early
SCOTLAND

This is modern 'Catriona' as selected by Scotland's most successful modern breeder, Jack Dunnett. It has bonny blue eyes and dominates its show classes. It has good disease resistance including partial double eelworm and slug resistance. 'Kestrel' is the best Caithness variety for flavour as far as I am concerned.

TUBER		RESISTANCE	
YIELD	7	FOLIAR BLIGHT	5
TUBER SHAPE	7	TUBER BLIGHT	3
EYE DEPTH	5	BLACKLEG	8
SKIN COLOUR	w/b	COMMON SCAB	4
FLESH COLOUR	3	POWDERY SCAB	5
DRY MATTER	4	SPRAING	2
RESISTANCE TO DISCOLOURING	8	POTATO CYST NEMATODE	pr
RESISTANCE TO DISINTEGRATION	5	SLUG	5

75

KING EDWARD
1902
Early maincrop
ENGLAND

This started out as 'Fellside Hero' in Northumberland, breeder 'unknown'. A merchant changed the name and linked it with the approaching coronation and it became England's best-known variety. The striking colouration helped develop its popularity but the consistent demand over the years is a testament to the eating and cooking qualities. The number of copycat varieties is another testament.

TUBER		RESISTANCE	
YIELD	6	FOLIAR BLIGHT	3
TUBER SHAPE	5	TUBER BLIGHT	4
EYE DEPTH	7	BLACKLEG	4
SKIN COLOUR	w/r	COMMON SCAB	7
FLESH COLOUR	4	POWDERY SCAB	7
DRY MATTER	6	SPRAING	6
RESISTANCE TO DISCOLOURING	5	POTATO CYST NEMATODE	s
RESISTANCE TO DISINTEGRATION	6	SLUG	6

KINGSTON
1981
Early maincrop
ENGLAND

This in my opinion was one of the first modern prepack varieties. It has huge yields, robustness, resistance to PCN and disease in general, brightness and 'mild' flavour. It was produced by the Maris station after the EU abolished variety prefixes.

TUBER		RESISTANCE	
YIELD	8	FOLIAR BLIGHT	4
TUBER SHAPE	4	TUBER BLIGHT	5
EYE DEPTH	7	BLACKLEG	5
SKIN COLOUR	w	COMMON SCAB	7
FLESH COLOUR	3	POWDERY SCAB	3
DRY MATTER	4	SPRAING	4
RESISTANCE TO DISCOLOURING	5	POTATO CYST NEMATODE	r
RESISTANCE TO DISINTEGRATION	7	SLUG	4

KONDOR

1984
Early maincrop
NETHERLANDS

'Kondor' is like a red version of 'Wilja', from which it is bred. It produces large, fairly disease-resistant tubers which cook well and suit the 'waxy' palate.

TUBER		RESISTANCE	
YIELD	8	FOLIAR BLIGHT	6
TUBER SHAPE	7	TUBER BLIGHT	6
EYE DEPTH	3	BLACKLEG	3
SKIN COLOUR	r	COMMON SCAB	6
FLESH COLOUR	6		5
DRY MATTER	5	SPRAING	1
RESISTANCE TO DISCOLOURING	5	POTATO CYST NEMATODE	s
RESISTANCE TO DISINTEGRATION	7	SLUG	3

LADY BALFOUR

2001
Early maincrop
SCOTLAND

This was bred by the Scottish Crop Research Institute with the needs of organic growing in mind. It was named after the Soil Association founder to encourage this concept. It has high yields, very good disease resistance (including partial double eelworm resistance) and what is described as 'vigour under low fertility conditions' – organic enthusiasts will not be flattered. Flavour is 'mild'.

TUBER		RESISTANCE	
YIELD	[8]	FOLIAR BLIGHT	8
TUBER SHAPE	6	TUBER BLIGHT	7
EYE DEPTH	6	BLACKLEG	7
SKIN COLOUR	w/r	COMMON SCAB	4
FLESH COLOUR	3	POWDERY SCAB	8
DRY MATTER	[3]	SPRAING	5
RESISTANCE TO DISCOLOURING	-	POTATO CYST NEMATODE	pr
RESISTANCE TO DISINTEGRATION	-	SLUG	3

LADY CHRISTL
1996
First early
NETHERLANDS

'Lady Christl' has become a garden favourite relatively quickly. It is very early and produces numerous, pretty, medium-sized, disease-resistant waxy tubers. It suits the sheltered, fertile garden environment. It is susceptible to foliar blight but has fairly good tuber blight resistance, which usually means it misses blight even in a wet summer.

TUBER		RESISTANCE	
YIELD	[7]	FOLIAR BLIGHT	2
TUBER SHAPE	6	TUBER BLIGHT	5
EYE DEPTH	5	BLACKLEG	5
SKIN COLOUR	y	COMMON SCAB	7
FLESH COLOUR	6	POWDERY SCAB	3
DRY MATTER	4	SPRAING	-
RESISTANCE TO DISCOLOURING	-	POTATO CYST NEMATODE	r
RESISTANCE TO DISINTEGRATION	-	SLUG	-

MAJESTIC
1911
Early maincrop
SCOTLAND

My hero, Archibald Findlay, produced this after his reputation as a breeder became overshadowed by doubt. It became the most grown variety in the UK in the twentieth century. It had very large yields and good resistance to disease for the time. It is consistently productive in a wide range of growing conditions and it stores well. Its large, white, slightly rough (to the modern eye) tubers are the epitome of potatoes for an older generation. Opinions on flavour have always varied.

TUBER		RESISTANCE	
YIELD	6	FOLIAR BLIGHT	4
TUBER SHAPE	6	TUBER BLIGHT	6
EYE DEPTH	7	BLACKLEG	-
SKIN COLOUR	w	COMMON SCAB	4
FLESH COLOUR	l	POWDERY SCAB	6
DRY MATTER	-	SPRAING	4
RESISTANCE TO DISCOLOURING	5	POTATO CYST NEMATODE	s
RESISTANCE TO DISINTEGRATION	7	SLUG	4

MALIN
1999
Early maincrop
IRELAND

This is an attractive TEAGASC 'Cara' × 'Estima' cross selection. Few details are available and the first photographs released did not flatter the variety. It was successfully exhibited in Ireland and visiting Welsh enthusiasts obtained a few – it is now seen quite frequently at shows, often with a misspelt label. The part-red colour pattern is between that of 'Amour' and 'Ambo'. 'Malin' is high yielding, waxy and stores well.

TUBER		RESISTANCE	
YIELD	[8]	FOLIAR BLIGHT	-
TUBER SHAPE	[7]	TUBER BLIGHT	-
EYE DEPTH	[8]	BLACKLEG	-
SKIN COLOUR	w/r	COMMON SCAB	[6]
FLESH COLOUR	[4]	POWDERY SCAB	-
DRY MATTER	-	SPRAING	-
RESISTANCE TO DISCOLOURING	-	POTATO CYST NEMATODE	S
RESISTANCE TO DISINTEGRATION	-	SLUG	-

MARFONA
1975
Second early
NETHERLANDS

'Marfona' is high yielding and suits a wide range of soils. It is the typical summer, waxy baker. The tubers are large, attractive and store well. It is the slug's favourite.

TUBER		RESISTANCE	
YIELD	8	FOLIAR BLIGHT	4
TUBER SHAPE	4	TUBER BLIGHT	4
EYE DEPTH	7	BLACKLEG	5
SKIN COLOUR	y	COMMON SCAB	5
FLESH COLOUR	5	POWDERY SCAB	5
DRY MATTER	3	SPRAING	6
RESISTANCE TO DISCOLOURING	6	POTATO CYST NEMATODE	S
RESISTANCE TO DISINTEGRATION	7	SLUG	1

79

MARIS BARD
1972
First early
ENGLAND

This was a PBI Cambridge variety which was the earliest early for a time. This title now belongs to varieties such as 'Rocket' and 'Swift'. 'Maris Bard' has high yield, good size and appearance, and good cooking characteristics and is now a well-established garden standard variety.

TUBER		RESISTANCE	
YIELD	8	FOLIAR BLIGHT	4
TUBER SHAPE	6	TUBER BLIGHT	4
EYE DEPTH	7	BLACKLEG	4
SKIN COLOUR	w	COMMON SCAB	5
FLESH COLOUR	2	POWDERY SCAB	3
DRY MATTER	4	SPRAING	2
RESISTANCE TO DISCOLOURING	7	POTATO CYST NEMATODE	S
RESISTANCE TO DISINTEGRATION	7	SLUG	-

MARIS PEER
1962
Second early
ENGLAND

This ageing PBI Cambridge canning variety has had a revival because of the demand for small, uniform, well-flavoured salad/boiling potatoes. Restaurants love their reliable firmness. To obtain the desired results the plants must be grown close together and kept earthed up. It is perhaps the most attractive potato plant known, with domed symmetry and strong purple flowers: a summer walk through a field of scented 'Maris Peer' flowers beats even the clichéd sunflower fantasy!

TUBER		RESISTANCE	
YIELD	5	FOLIAR BLIGHT	4
TUBER SHAPE	4	TUBER BLIGHT	4
EYE DEPTH	8	BLACKLEG	4
SKIN COLOUR	w	COMMON SCAB	5
FLESH COLOUR	3	POWDERY SCAB	6
DRY MATTER	5	SPRAING	3
RESISTANCE TO DISCOLOURING	8	POTATO CYST NEMATODE	S
RESISTANCE TO DISINTEGRATION	8	SLUG	4

MARIS PIPER
1964
Early maincrop
ENGLAND

'Maris Piper' was the first commercially successful eelworm-resistant variety and still dominates field production in the UK today. It pre-dates Plant Variety Rights and seed is cheap. It will be difficult to displace for it has decent yields, top flavour and the best ever frying characteristics. It is the chip-shop favourite. It is not very garden friendly, being prone to scab, slug damage and the production of many small tubers.

TUBER		RESISTANCE	
YIELD	7	FOLIAR BLIGHT	4
TUBER SHAPE	4	TUBER BLIGHT	5
EYE DEPTH	8	BLACKLEG	5
SKIN COLOUR	w	COMMON SCAB	1
FLESH COLOUR	2	POWDERY SCAB	3
DRY MATTER	7	SPRAING	5
RESISTANCE TO DISCOLOURING	6	POTATO CYST NEMATODE	r
RESISTANCE TO DISINTEGRATION	5	SLUG	2

MARITIEMA
1991
Second early
NETHERLANDS

This is a rare but interesting variety. It has few faults except blight susceptibility and it is double eelworm resistant.

TUBER		RESISTANCE	
YIELD	[7]	FOLIAR BLIGHT	2
TUBER SHAPE	5	TUBER BLIGHT	3
EYE DEPTH	6	BLACKLEG	7
SKIN COLOUR	y	COMMON SCAB	6
FLESH COLOUR	5	POWDERY SCAB	6
DRY MATTER	[6]	SPRAING	7
RESISTANCE TO DISCOLOURING	-	POTATO CYST NEMATODE	7
RESISTANCE TO DISINTEGRATION	-	SLUG	5

MAXINE
1993
Early maincrop
SCOTLAND

This is Jack Dunnett's most successful red. It has bright colouration and is attractive, productive, firm and waxy. It is easily the most successful exhibition red at the moment. It has double eelworm resistance.

TUBER		RESISTANCE	
YIELD	7	FOLIAR BLIGHT	4
TUBER SHAPE	5	TUBER BLIGHT	3
EYE DEPTH	5	BLACKLEG	7
SKIN COLOUR	r	COMMON SCAB	3
FLESH COLOUR	3	POWDERY SCAB	7
DRY MATTER	4	SPRAING	I
RESISTANCE TO DISCOLOURING	6	POTATO CYST NEMATODE	r
RESISTANCE TO DISINTEGRATION	7	SLUG	2

MERLIN
1997
Early maincrop
SCOTLAND

This is a rare, high-yielding Jack Dunnett variety, a red-eyed selection from a 'Cara' cross, but it lacks blight and eelworm resistance. It stores very well.

TUBER		RESISTANCE	
YIELD	[8]	FOLIAR BLIGHT	3
TUBER SHAPE	4	TUBER BLIGHT	4
EYE DEPTH	6	BLACKLEG	8
SKIN COLOUR	w/r	COMMON SCAB	5
FLESH COLOUR	3	POWDERY SCAB	5
DRY MATTER	5	SPRAING	-
RESISTANCE TO DISCOLOURING	7	POTATO CYST NEMATODE	s
RESISTANCE TO DISINTEGRATION	-	SLUG	-

MIDAS

1996
Early maincrop
ENGLAND

This is a PBI Cambridge/Cygnet PB variety, very much in the 'Maris Piper' mould but with better scab, slug, blight and virus resistance and it has double eelworm resistance. It has excellent flavour, fries very well and cooks well enough to be classed 'general purpose'. It has not taken off commercially because it costs more than 'Maris Piper' and it is struggling to match yields.

TUBER		RESISTANCE	
YIELD	6	FOLIAR BLIGHT	8
TUBER SHAPE	5	TUBER BLIGHT	4
EYE DEPTH	5	BLACKLEG	5
SKIN COLOUR	w	COMMON SCAB	5
FLESH COLOUR	6	POWDERY SCAB	4
DRY MATTER	9	SPRAING	1
RESISTANCE TO DISCOLOURING	6	POTATO CYST NEMATODE	r
RESISTANCE TO DISINTEGRATION	5	SLUG	4

MILVA

1990s
Second early
NETHERLANDS

'Milva' is a modern Dutch, disease-resistant, prepack type. A little English-grown organic seed has been available recently.

TUBER		RESISTANCE	
YIELD	[8]	FOLIAR BLIGHT	[6]
TUBER SHAPE	[5]	TUBER BLIGHT	[5]
EYE DEPTH	[7]	BLACKLEG	[7]
SKIN COLOUR	y	COMMON SCAB	[7]
FLESH COLOUR	[8]	POWDERY SCAB	-
DRY MATTER	[4]	SPRAING	-
RESISTANCE TO DISCOLOURING	[7]	POTATO CYST NEMATODE	r?
RESISTANCE TO DISINTEGRATION	[7]	SLUG	-

MIMI
2002
First early
SCOTLAND

'Mimi' represents a new direction for Jack Dunnett. It is a red first early which produces lots of small 'cherry' salad/boil-whole potatoes. It is said to be common scab resistant but facts and figures from large-scale trials are not available. It came out top in a small-scale taste test of new varieties conducted with a group of horticultural journalists. The seed tubers are very small.

TUBER		RESISTANCE	
YIELD	-	FOLIAR BLIGHT	-
TUBER SHAPE	-	TUBER BLIGHT	-
EYE DEPTH	-	BLACKLEG	-
SKIN COLOUR	r	COMMON SCAB	
FLESH COLOUR	-	POWDERY SCAB	
DRY MATTER	-	SPRAING	-
RESISTANCE TO DISCOLOURING	-	POTATO CYST NEMATODE	-
RESISTANCE TO DISINTEGRATION	-	SLUG	-

MINERVA
1988
First early
NETHERLANDS

This variety produces few but large tubers. They have good appearance and some disease resistance but are prone to blight and spraing.

TUBER		RESISTANCE	
YIELD	8	FOLIAR BLIGHT	4
TUBER SHAPE	4	TUBER BLIGHT	1
EYE DEPTH	5	BLACKLEG	3
SKIN COLOUR	w	COMMON SCAB	6
FLESH COLOUR	4	POWDERY SCAB	5
DRY MATTER	4	SPRAING	2
RESISTANCE TO DISCOLOURING	7	POTATO CYST NEMATODE	r
RESISTANCE TO DISINTEGRATION	7	SLUG	-

MORENE
1983
Early maincrop
NETHERLANDS

'Morene' produces large, clean, high dry matter tubers. They are used commercially for crisps, bakers and chips. Those who used to seek out 'Record' and are now finding it difficult to find would probably like this one. It has a disease-resistant, trouble-free reputation.

TUBER		RESISTANCE	
YIELD	8	FOLIAR BLIGHT	6
TUBER SHAPE	6	TUBER BLIGHT	6
EYE DEPTH	7	BLACKLEG	2
SKIN COLOUR	w	COMMON SCAB	7
FLESH COLOUR	3	POWDERY SCAB	-
DRY MATTER	7	SPRAING	3
RESISTANCE TO DISCOLOURING	6	POTATO CYST NEMATODE	r
RESISTANCE TO DISINTEGRATION	5	SLUG	5

NADINE
1987
Second early
SCOTLAND

This was Jack Dunnett's first major success as an independent breeder. It is grown all over the world. Although not drought tolerant, it does very well in irrigated desert soils. Indeed it has an unofficial yield record in Australia. The tubers are pretty and waxy and boil well. 'Nadine' and its sister variety 'Sherine' have had unprecedented showbench success. 'Nadine' has double eelworm resistance.

TUBER		RESISTANCE	
YIELD	7	FOLIAR BLIGHT	6
TUBER SHAPE	4	TUBER BLIGHT	4
EYE DEPTH	8	BLACKLEG	3
SKIN COLOUR	w	COMMON SCAB	7
FLESH COLOUR	3	POWDERY SCAB	3
DRY MATTER	2	SPRAING	6
RESISTANCE TO DISCOLOURING	8	POTATO CYST NEMATODE	r
RESISTANCE TO DISINTEGRATION	6	SLUG	4

NAVAN

1987
Late maincrop
NORTHERN IRELAND

This is a product of the Northern Ireland Plant Breeding Station. It was bred from and designed to replace 'Maris Piper'. It fries well and has excellent flavour. It has the looked-for yield, high dry matter and at least some of the disease resistance. Its main problems apart from seed cost are late maturity and susceptibility to spraing.

TUBER		RESISTANCE	
YIELD	8	FOLIAR BLIGHT	5
TUBER SHAPE	4	TUBER BLIGHT	4
EYE DEPTH	6	BLACKLEG	6
SKIN COLOUR	w	COMMON SCAB	4
FLESH COLOUR	3	POWDERY SCAB	5
DRY MATTER	8	SPRAING	1
RESISTANCE TO DISCOLOURING	7	POTATO CYST NEMATODE	r
RESISTANCE TO DISINTEGRATION	5	SLUG	4

NICOLA

1973
Early maincrop
GERMANY

Close-grown 'Nicola', 'Charlotte' and 'Maris Peer' have become popular in recent decades to supply the demand for small, firm, waxy salad/boiling potatoes with flavour. 'Nicola' is yellow fleshed and eelworm resistant, and grows long if given space. It used to be blight resistant but is less so now as blight has evolved. Many new potato varieties are 'designed' for its niche but usually lack the flavour.

TUBER		RESISTANCE	
YIELD	[7]	FOLIAR BLIGHT	2
TUBER SHAPE	7	TUBER BLIGHT	3
EYE DEPTH	6	BLACKLEG	5
SKIN COLOUR	y	COMMON SCAB	6
FLESH COLOUR	6	POWDERY SCAB	5
DRY MATTER	[5]	SPRAING	4
RESISTANCE TO DISCOLOURING	[7]	POTATO CYST NEMATODE	r
RESISTANCE TO DISINTEGRATION	[8]	SLUG	6

ORLA

*c.*2000
First early
IRELAND

This TEAGASC variety is the most blight-resistant early ever produced. This is important as blight is now more virulent and onset of infection is earlier. It is attractive and has good resistance to disease, with the exception of eelworm. It also has good early yields, particularly if seed is chitted. Unusually for an early it has long dormancy and stores quite well. It is a good variety for second cropping.

TUBER		RESISTANCE	
YIELD	6	FOLIAR BLIGHT	8
TUBER SHAPE	5	TUBER BLIGHT	8
EYE DEPTH	6	BLACKLEG	6
SKIN COLOUR	w	COMMON SCAB	5
FLESH COLOUR	4	POWDERY SCAB	4
DRY MATTER	3	SPRAING	5
RESISTANCE TO DISCOLOURING	[7]	POTATO CYST NEMATODE	s
RESISTANCE TO DISINTEGRATION	[6]	SLUG	-

OSPREY

1999
Second early
SCOTLAND

This is another attractive Jack Dunnett variety. It is like a pink-eyed 'Kestrel' (which is a parent), with higher yields and some of the disease resistance, including partial double eelworm resistance. Despite low to medium dry matter content it has quite a floury texture.

TUBER		RESISTANCE	
YIELD	[8]	FOLIAR BLIGHT	4
TUBER SHAPE	5	TUBER BLIGHT	5
EYE DEPTH	5	BLACKLEG	9
SKIN COLOUR	w/r	COMMON SCAB	6
FLESH COLOUR	3	POWDERY SCAB	6
DRY MATTER	[5]	SPRAING	6
RESISTANCE TO DISCOLOURING	-	POTATO CYST NEMATODE	pr
RESISTANCE TO DISINTEGRATION	-	SLUG	5

PENTA

1983
Second early
NETHERLANDS

This is an attractive, pink-eyed variety which, just for a change, is not a selection from a 'Cara' cross ('Estima' is a parent). It is rare but occasionally sought by showbench enthusiasts. It is high yielding and fairly disease resistant.

TUBER		RESISTANCE	
YIELD	8	FOLIAR BLIGHT	6
TUBER SHAPE	4	TUBER BLIGHT	5
EYE DEPTH	4	BLACKLEG	1
SKIN COLOUR	w/r	COMMON SCAB	7
FLESH COLOUR	5	POWDERY SCAB	3
DRY MATTER	5	SPRAING	5
RESISTANCE TO DISCOLOURING	7	POTATO CYST NEMATODE	r
RESISTANCE TO DISINTEGRATION	7	SLUG	5

PENTLAND CROWN

1959
Early maincrop
SCOTLAND

'Pentland Crown' was the first 'Pentland' variety (from Pentlandfield Station, Edinburgh) to have an impact – the varieties came out in alphabetical order. It displaced 'Majestic' as the most common variety in the UK. 'Pentland Crown' is robust, drought resistant, disease resistant and very productive – it even produces long stolons to fill adjacent gaps in the row. It was the first variety to be banned from a supermarket chain for lack of flavour. Now rare.

TUBER		RESISTANCE	
YIELD	8	FOLIAR BLIGHT	3
TUBER SHAPE	6	TUBER BLIGHT	5
EYE DEPTH	7	BLACKLEG	7
SKIN COLOUR	w	COMMON SCAB	7
FLESH COLOUR	2	POWDERY SCAB	4
DRY MATTER	6	SPRAING	3
RESISTANCE TO DISCOLOURING	3	POTATO CYST NEMATODE	s
RESISTANCE TO DISINTEGRATION	6	SLUG	4

PENTLAND DELL

1961
Early maincrop
SCOTLAND

This is another well-known, high-yielding 'Pentland'. It was launched as the first blight-immune variety. Despite the disease evolving fairly quickly to make this nonsense, 'Pentland Dell' has a huge acreage – its large tubers are good for general-purpose ware, bakers, frozen chips and up-market crisps. The foliage often looks unpromising and scruffy but the size and yield surprise. It has some slug resistance.

TUBER		RESISTANCE	
YIELD	7	FOLIAR BLIGHT	6
TUBER SHAPE	7	TUBER BLIGHT	5
EYE DEPTH	7	BLACKLEG	4
SKIN COLOUR	w	COMMON SCAB	5
FLESH COLOUR	3	POWDERY SCAB	7
DRY MATTER	7	SPRAING	I
RESISTANCE TO DISCOLOURING	4	POTATO CYST NEMATODE	S
RESISTANCE TO DISINTEGRATION	5	SLUG	6

PENTLAND HAWK

1966
Early maincrop
SCOTLAND

'Pentland Hawk' has slightly lower yields than the common maincrop 'Pentland' varieties but it has better culinary characteristics. It is one of the best varieties for storing produced in more recent times.

TUBER		RESISTANCE	
YIELD	6	FOLIAR BLIGHT	4
TUBER SHAPE	5	TUBER BLIGHT	6
EYE DEPTH	8	BLACKLEG	-
SKIN COLOUR	w	COMMON SCAB	6
FLESH COLOUR	3	POWDERY SCAB	5
DRY MATTER	6	SPRAING	I
RESISTANCE TO DISCOLOURING	6	POTATO CYST NEMATODE	S
RESISTANCE TO DISINTEGRATION	8	SLUG	-

PENTLAND IVORY

1966
Early maincrop
SCOTLAND

This is the quality 'Pentland', but it is now very rare because its yield is very variable and unpredictable. It has survived because of enthusiasm for the variety by a few individuals in Ireland.

TUBER		RESISTANCE	
YIELD	[6]	FOLIAR BLIGHT	4
TUBER SHAPE	3	TUBER BLIGHT	7
EYE DEPTH	5	BLACKLEG	-
SKIN COLOUR	w	COMMON SCAB	6
FLESH COLOUR	2	POWDERY SCAB	6
DRY MATTER	7	SPRAING	1
RESISTANCE TO DISCOLOURING	6	POTATO CYST NEMATODE	s
RESISTANCE TO DISINTEGRATION	7	SLUG	5

PENTLAND JAVELIN

1968
First early
SCOTLAND

'Pentland Javelin' is a showbench-quality early with good flavour, tuber number and disease resistance. Quality needs time to develop and it is regarded as a bit on the late side nowadays. It was bred by a certain young Dr Jack Dunnett when he worked at Pentlandfield.

TUBER		RESISTANCE	
YIELD	6	FOLIAR BLIGHT	4
TUBER SHAPE	3	TUBER BLIGHT	2
EYE DEPTH	8	BLACKLEG	5
SKIN COLOUR	w	COMMON SCAB	6
FLESH COLOUR	1	POWDERY SCAB	[2]
DRY MATTER	4	SPRAING	2
RESISTANCE TO DISCOLOURING	6	POTATO CYST NEMATODE	r
RESISTANCE TO DISINTEGRATION	7	SLUG	-

PENTLAND SQUIRE
1970
Early maincrop
SCOTLAND

'Pentland Squire' is very similar to 'Pentland Dell' but the tuber is shorter and the yield is sometimes higher. This was one of the few 'Pentland' varieties subject to Plant Variety Rights payments and the maintainer always asked for high prices. Demand fell away. These payments have now lapsed and it will be interesting to see if available quantities increase.

TUBER		RESISTANCE	
YIELD	8	FOLIAR BLIGHT	6
TUBER SHAPE	4	TUBER BLIGHT	5
EYE DEPTH	5	BLACKLEG	4
SKIN COLOUR	w	COMMON SCAB	6
FLESH COLOUR	2	POWDERY SCAB	7
DRY MATTER	7	SPRAING	3
RESISTANCE TO DISCOLOURING	5	POTATO CYST NEMATODE	s
RESISTANCE TO DISINTEGRATION	4	SLUG	5

PICASSO
1992
Early maincrop
NETHERLANDS

This is a popular, modern, eelworm-resistant variety with striking red eyes aimed at the 'King Edward'/'Cara' market. 'Cara' was a parent. The yield is massive and the tubers store well. It would suit the substantial group of gardeners who want 'mild', waxy, firm, boiling potatoes.

TUBER		RESISTANCE	
YIELD	9	FOLIAR BLIGHT	5
TUBER SHAPE	5	TUBER BLIGHT	6
EYE DEPTH	5	BLACKLEG	5
SKIN COLOUR	w/r	COMMON SCAB	7
FLESH COLOUR	4	POWDERY SCAB	3
DRY MATTER	2	SPRAING	1
RESISTANCE TO DISCOLOURING	5	POTATO CYST NEMATODE	r
RESISTANCE TO DISINTEGRATION	7	SLUG	3

PINK FIR APPLE
1850
Late maincrop
FRANCE? GERMANY?

A century ago, Suttons had four 'Fir Apple's – large white, small white, red and pink, origin unstated. The pink survived, kept going for decades by British enthusiasts. It was rare, but there is now plenty of certified seed. The tubers are knobbly and impossible to peel, and should be cooked whole. They are firm and delightful hot or cold. They fry surprisingly well and decadence is making chips from individual tubers!

TUBER		RESISTANCE	
YIELD	-	FOLIAR BLIGHT	-
TUBER SHAPE	[9]	TUBER BLIGHT	-
EYE DEPTH	3	BLACKLEG	-
SKIN COLOUR	P	COMMON SCAB	-
FLESH COLOUR	7	POWDERY SCAB	-
DRY MATTER	[5]	SPRAING	-
RESISTANCE TO DISCOLOURING	-	POTATO CYST NEMATODE	S
RESISTANCE TO DISINTEGRATION	[8]	SLUG	-

POMEROY
2001
Late maincrop
NORTHERN IRELAND

This won a tasting test of new varieties overwhelmingly at a trade conference. It is very good but the variety is new and official figures don't yet exist. It is very blight, scab and blackleg resistant but lateness and possible susceptibility to spraing may be its undoing. Yields are excellent.

TUBER		RESISTANCE	
YIELD	[8]	FOLIAR BLIGHT	[7]
TUBER SHAPE	[5]	TUBER BLIGHT	[7]
EYE DEPTH	-	BLACKLEG	[7]
SKIN COLOUR	w	COMMON SCAB	[7]
FLESH COLOUR	[5]	POWDERY SCAB	-
DRY MATTER	[7]	SPRAING	[!?]
RESISTANCE TO DISCOLOURING	-	POTATO CYST NEMATODE	r
RESISTANCE TO DISINTEGRATION	-	SLUG	-

PREMIERE
1979
First early
NETHERLANDS

This has been quite a popular, disease-resistant early. It has good flavour with dry, yellow flesh which will fry. It is one of the few earlies with a reputation for blight resistance. However, this reputation has become disputed by claims that there are now strains around to which 'Premiere' is susceptible.

TUBER		RESISTANCE	
YIELD	7	FOLIAR BLIGHT	6
TUBER SHAPE	5	TUBER BLIGHT	5
EYE DEPTH	5	BLACKLEG	1
SKIN COLOUR	y	COMMON SCAB	5
FLESH COLOUR	7	POWDERY SCAB	5
DRY MATTER	6	SPRAING	8
RESISTANCE TO DISCOLOURING	8	POTATO CYST NEMATODE	r
RESISTANCE TO DISINTEGRATION	6	SLUG	-

PROVENTO
1990s
Early maincrop?
NETHERLANDS

This variety received unwelcome publicity because, allegedly, seed of it carried ring rot into the UK for the first time. It is being promoted as a disease-resistant maincrop suitable for organic production but available information is confusing.

TUBER		RESISTANCE	
YIELD	[8]	FOLIAR BLIGHT	[5]
TUBER SHAPE	[3]	TUBER BLIGHT	[7]
EYE DEPTH	[8]	BLACKLEG	[6]
SKIN COLOUR	y	COMMON SCAB	[5]
FLESH COLOUR	[6]	POWDERY SCAB	[5]
DRY MATTER	[6]	SPRAING	[8]
RESISTANCE TO DISCOLOURING	[7]	POTATO CYST NEMATODE	s
RESISTANCE TO DISINTEGRATION	[5]	SLUG	-

PRINCESS
1990s
First early
GERMANY

This is a very new variety which will be difficult to find. Initial reports praise and highlight its use as a salad potato. It gained a Royal Horticultural Society salad potato award very early in its development.

TUBER		RESISTANCE	
YIELD	[6]	FOLIAR BLIGHT	[5]
TUBER SHAPE	[5]	TUBER BLIGHT	[5]
EYE DEPTH	[7]	BLACKLEG	[5]
SKIN COLOUR	y	COMMON SCAB	[6]
FLESH COLOUR	[7]	POWDERY SCAB	-
DRY MATTER	[4]	SPRAING	-
RESISTANCE TO DISCOLOURING	-	POTATO CYST NEMATODE	r
RESISTANCE TO DISINTEGRATION	[7]	SLUG	-

RATTE [ASPARGES]
1872
Early maincrop
DENMARK? FRANCE?

This has flavour and cooking qualities reminiscent of those of 'Pink Fir Apple'. 'Ratte' is earlier, often more productive, has fewer knobbly bits, shorter stems and nicer flowers. It is now a 'classic' of French cuisine, although it was probably 'Asparges' in Denmark first. Have fun telling a French chef this!

TUBER		RESISTANCE	
YIELD	-	FOLIAR BLIGHT	-
TUBER SHAPE	[9]	TUBER BLIGHT	-
EYE DEPTH	-	BLACKLEG	-
SKIN COLOUR	y	COMMON SCAB	-
FLESH COLOUR	[7]	POWDERY SCAB	-
DRY MATTER	[4]	SPRAING	-
RESISTANCE TO DISCOLOURING	-	POTATO CYST NEMATODE	s
RESISTANCE TO DISINTEGRATION	[9]	SLUG	-

RECORD

1932
Early maincrop
NETHERLANDS

This heavy-duty potato was the favourite of organic guru Lawrence Hills. It has high dry matter with real flavour and it used to be the mainstay of the UK crisp industry until US takeover followed by saturation advertising convinced our children that pale gold rather than deep gold crisps were the best. 'Record' is now rare but a little is still grown for gardeners. It is great mashed, steamed, fried or roasted.

TUBER		RESISTANCE	
YIELD	5	FOLIAR BLIGHT	5
TUBER SHAPE	4	TUBER BLIGHT	6
EYE DEPTH	5	BLACKLEG	2
SKIN COLOUR	y	COMMON SCAB	6
FLESH COLOUR	6	POWDERY SCAB	7
DRY MATTER	9	SPRAING	8
RESISTANCE TO DISCOLOURING	5	POTATO CYST NEMATODE	s
RESISTANCE TO DISINTEGRATION	2	SLUG	4

RED CARA

1976
Late maincrop
IRELAND

This is a red sport of 'Cara' which can occasionally revert back.

TUBER		RESISTANCE	
YIELD	[8]	FOLIAR BLIGHT	6
TUBER SHAPE	3	TUBER BLIGHT	7
EYE DEPTH	6	BLACKLEG	4
SKIN COLOUR	r	COMMON SCAB	6
FLESH COLOUR	3	POWDERY SCAB	3
DRY MATTER	3	SPRAING	3
RESISTANCE TO DISCOLOURING	7	POTATO CYST NEMATODE	r
RESISTANCE TO DISINTEGRATION	7	SLUG	4

RED DUKE OF YORK
1942
First early
NETHERLANDS

This was first found in a Dutch crop of 'Duke of York' ('Eersteling' in the Netherlands). It has deep red skin colour, is more vigorous than white 'Duke's and has spectacular foliage with blue 'centres'. With great flavour and large tubers this is one of the few heritage varieties to gain a little modern commercial success in the form of Waitrose summer bakers and Marks & Spencer heritage crisps.

TUBER		RESISTANCE	
YIELD	4	FOLIAR BLIGHT	[3]
TUBER SHAPE	6	TUBER BLIGHT	[3]
EYE DEPTH	7	BLACKLEG	-
SKIN COLOUR	r	COMMON SCAB	[5]
FLESH COLOUR	5	POWDERY SCAB	-
DRY MATTER	3-6	SPRAING	[6]
RESISTANCE TO DISCOLOURING	9	POTATO CYST NEMATODE	s
RESISTANCE TO DISINTEGRATION	9-5	SLUG	-

REDGEM
1996
Early maincrop
SCOTLAND

This Jack Dunnett variety looks like a smooth 'Desiree' and cooks like 'Maris Piper', both varieties being in its breeding. It has partial double eelworm resistance.

TUBER		RESISTANCE	
YIELD	[8]	FOLIAR BLIGHT	3
TUBER SHAPE	5	TUBER BLIGHT	4
EYE DEPTH	9	BLACKLEG	8
SKIN COLOUR	r	COMMON SCAB	2
FLESH COLOUR	3	POWDERY SCAB	-
DRY MATTER	6	SPRAING	-
RESISTANCE TO DISCOLOURING	6	POTATO CYST NEMATODE	pr
RESISTANCE TO DISINTEGRATION	-	SLUG	-

RED KING EDWARD
1916
Early maincrop
UK

This is a rare red sport of 'King Edward' which is now back in production. Some enthusiasts rate it as an improvement on the original. It used to be marketed as 'Red Kings'.

TUBER		RESISTANCE	
YIELD	[6]	FOLIAR BLIGHT	[3]
TUBER SHAPE	[5]	TUBER BLIGHT	[4]
EYE DEPTH	[7]	BLACKLEG	[4]
SKIN COLOUR	r	COMMON SCAB	[7]
FLESH COLOUR	[4]	POWDERY SCAB	[7]
DRY MATTER	[6]	SPRAING	[6]
RESISTANCE TO DISCOLOURING	[5]	POTATO CYST NEMATODE	s
RESISTANCE TO DISINTEGRATION	[6]	SLUG	[6]

REMARKA
1992
Early maincrop
NETHERLANDS

This variety has very good all-round disease resistance. It is an organic gardening favourite because of its blight resistance, good flavour and good cooking characteristics. It produces relatively few but large tubers suitable for baking. They are very prone to growth cracks and hollow heart. For best results 'Remarka' needs good water supply and careful weeding.

TUBER		RESISTANCE	
YIELD	[8]	FOLIAR BLIGHT	[8]
TUBER SHAPE	[5]	TUBER BLIGHT	[7]
EYE DEPTH	[8]	BLACKLEG	-
SKIN COLOUR	y	COMMON SCAB	[5]
FLESH COLOUR	[5]	POWDERY SCAB	-
DRY MATTER	[7]	SPRAING	-
RESISTANCE TO DISCOLOURING	[8]	POTATO CYST NEMATODE	r
RESISTANCE TO DISINTEGRATION	-	SLUG	-

ROCKET
1987
First early
ENGLAND

This PBI Cambridge variety is among the earliest to crop. It produces large crops of uniform, attractive, exhibition-quality, round tubers. It does not mature well – it can go hollow and split. It has double eelworm resistance but is very prone to tuber blight. The flavour is exceptionally 'mild'.

TUBER		RESISTANCE	
YIELD	9	FOLIAR BLIGHT	4
TUBER SHAPE	2	TUBER BLIGHT	1
EYE DEPTH	6	BLACKLEG	6
SKIN COLOUR	w	COMMON SCAB	5
FLESH COLOUR	1	POWDERY SCAB	3
DRY MATTER	4	SPRAING	5
RESISTANCE TO DISCOLOURING	8	POTATO CYST NEMATODE	r
RESISTANCE TO DISINTEGRATION	6	SLUG	-

ROMANO
1978
Early maincrop
NETHERLANDS

This variety was supposed to replace 'Desiree', its parent. 'Romano' is more uniform and less prone to scab. It does not have the strong flavour of 'Desiree' or its drought resistance but it does have better blight and slug resistance. The wet weather of more recent years has led to an increase in gardening use of 'Romano'.

TUBER		RESISTANCE	
YIELD	7	FOLIAR BLIGHT	7
TUBER SHAPE	3	TUBER BLIGHT	5
EYE DEPTH	6	BLACKLEG	5
SKIN COLOUR	r	COMMON SCAB	5
FLESH COLOUR	3	POWDERY SCAB	5
DRY MATTER	5	SPRAING	7
RESISTANCE TO DISCOLOURING	6	POTATO CYST NEMATODE	s
RESISTANCE TO DISINTEGRATION	6	SLUG	6

ROOSTER
1993
Early maincrop
IRELAND

This TEAGASC variety has quickly become a major variety in Ireland, rivalling 'Kerr's Pink', despite being subject to Plant Variety Rights. It is gathering a word-of-mouth reputation for very good flavour among gardeners and farm shop customers in the UK, despite being classified by NIAB as a specialist crisping variety.

TUBER		RESISTANCE	
YIELD	7	FOLIAR BLIGHT	4
TUBER SHAPE	5	TUBER BLIGHT	5
EYE DEPTH	5	BLACKLEG	6
SKIN COLOUR	r	COMMON SCAB	5
FLESH COLOUR	6	POWDERY SCAB	4
DRY MATTER	8	SPRAING	8
RESISTANCE TO DISCOLOURING	5	POTATO CYST NEMATODE	s
RESISTANCE TO DISINTEGRATION	6	SLUG	3

ROSEVAL
1950
Early maincrop
FRANCE

This is a very attractive, classic, deep red salad potato with yellow flesh often with a pink blush. Cooking quality and flavour are excellent. It has striking foliage with ruby-red stems. 'Roseval' is common in France but fairly rare in the UK.

TUBER		RESISTANCE	
YIELD	-	FOLIAR BLIGHT	-
TUBER SHAPE	[6]	TUBER BLIGHT	-
EYE DEPTH	[6]	BLACKLEG	-
SKIN COLOUR	r	COMMON SCAB	-
FLESH COLOUR	[8]	POWDERY SCAB	-
DRY MATTER	-	SPRAING	-
RESISTANCE TO DISCOLOURING	-	POTATO CYST NEMATODE	s
RESISTANCE TO DISINTEGRATION	-	SLUG	-

ROYAL KIDNEY

1899
Second early
SCOTLAND

Archibald Findlay deliberately chose a name to compete with 'International Kidney'. 'Royal Kidney' is a good waxy salad/boiling potato and is genuinely early. At one time the 'Royal Kidney' crop from Majorca and England was greater than that of 'Jersey Royal'. These imported harbingers of spring always had a mystique and debates about their flavour, texture and cooking qualities can get lively.

TUBER		RESISTANCE	
YIELD	-	FOLIAR BLIGHT	[4]
TUBER SHAPE	5	TUBER BLIGHT	[3]
EYE DEPTH	7	BLACKLEG	-
SKIN COLOUR	y	COMMON SCAB	-
FLESH COLOUR	5	POWDERY SCAB	-
DRY MATTER	[3]	SPRAING	[7]
RESISTANCE TO DISCOLOURING	[8]	POTATO CYST NEMATODE	S
RESISTANCE TO DISINTEGRATION	[7]	SLUG	-

RUSSET BURBANK

1875
Early maincrop
USA

This was bred by Luther Burbank of Maine and became the 'Idaho' potato, which has dominated the American market for more than a century. It is dry and starchy and used extensively for processing. A large acreage is grown for frozen fries wherever McDonald's trades.

TUBER		RESISTANCE	
YIELD	6	FOLIAR BLIGHT	3
TUBER SHAPE	9	TUBER BLIGHT	I
EYE DEPTH	3	BLACKLEG	-
SKIN COLOUR	w/ru	COMMON SCAB	8
FLESH COLOUR	3	POWDERY SCAB	-
DRY MATTER	6	SPRAING	2
RESISTANCE TO DISCOLOURING	-	POTATO CYST NEMATODE	S
RESISTANCE TO DISINTEGRATION	-	SLUG	4

SANTE

1983
Early maincrop
NETHERLANDS

This is a robust, disease-resistant variety with tubers like flattened pebbles. It was the first commercially important variety to be double eelworm resistant. It has dominated European organic growing.

TUBER		RESISTANCE	
YIELD	7	FOLIAR BLIGHT	7
TUBER SHAPE	3	TUBER BLIGHT	6
EYE DEPTH	6	BLACKLEG	3
SKIN COLOUR	y	COMMON SCAB	6
FLESH COLOUR	5	POWDERY SCAB	8
DRY MATTER	6	SPRAING	6
RESISTANCE TO DISCOLOURING	6	POTATO CYST NEMATODE	r
RESISTANCE TO DISINTEGRATION	6	SLUG	5

SARPO MIRA

2003
Late maincrop
HUNGARY

This is the first of a raft of 'Sarpo' varieties produced by the Sarvari family. It is the product of many years of Soviet-style long-term breeding followed by a few decades of private family effort with some recent Western pressure to improve appearance. The (conventional) breeding is complex and very sophisticated. 'Sarpo' varieties are vigorous, nutritious, extraordinarily disease (blight!) resistant and capable of growing in a wide range of conditions.

TUBER		RESISTANCE	
YIELD	[8]	FOLIAR BLIGHT	9
TUBER SHAPE	[6]	TUBER BLIGHT	9
EYE DEPTH	[5]	BLACKLEG	-
SKIN COLOUR	r	COMMON SCAB	-
FLESH COLOUR	[4]	POWDERY SCAB	-
DRY MATTER	[8]	SPRAING	-
RESISTANCE TO DISCOLOURING	-	POTATO CYST NEMATODE	s
RESISTANCE TO DISINTEGRATION	-	SLUG	-

SATURNA
1964
Second early/early maincrop
NETHERLANDS

'Saturna' is one of Europe's best frying potatoes. It is also tasty. It has a small but enthusiastic following but is becoming difficult to find as horticultural outlets become more and more committed to higher-yielding salad/boiling varieties. It has useful disease resistance.

TUBER		RESISTANCE	
YIELD	5	FOLIAR BLIGHT	4
TUBER SHAPE	3	TUBER BLIGHT	5
EYE DEPTH	4	BLACKLEG	-
SKIN COLOUR	y	COMMON SCAB	8
FLESH COLOUR	7	POWDERY SCAB	-
DRY MATTER	9	SPRAING	7
RESISTANCE TO DISCOLOURING	-	POTATO CYST NEMATODE	r
RESISTANCE TO DISINTEGRATION	-	SLUG	4

SAXON
1992
Second early
ENGLAND

After hearing me decry modern varieties for lack of flavour, a promoter insisted I tried 'Saxon'. It is very pleasant and creamy. I ate my words (as well). It is an attractive, high-yielding, disease-resistant, general-purpose variety from PBI Cambridge (now Cygnet PB). To avoid gaps, 'Saxon' needs to be planted in mild conditions.

TUBER		RESISTANCE	
YIELD	7	FOLIAR BLIGHT	3
TUBER SHAPE	4	TUBER BLIGHT	4
EYE DEPTH	6	BLACKLEG	8
SKIN COLOUR	w	COMMON SCAB	5
FLESH COLOUR	3	POWDERY SCAB	6
DRY MATTER	4	SPRAING	7
RESISTANCE TO DISCOLOURING	6	POTATO CYST NEMATODE	r
RESISTANCE TO DISINTEGRATION	6	SLUG	3

SHANNON

1990s
Early maincrop
IRELAND

This is a pretty, TEAGASC, waxy red aimed at the prepack market. 'Cara' is a parent. It has very high yields but with unimpressive disease resistance and low dry matter it ignites my prejudices. Like 'Malin', it was spotted by Welsh exhibitors in Ireland. It had an immediate impact at UK shows, was picked up by one of the catalogues and now has a small but enthusiastic following, who claim it is very good to eat.

TUBER		RESISTANCE	
YIELD	[9]	FOLIAR BLIGHT	3
TUBER SHAPE	6	TUBER BLIGHT	5
EYE DEPTH	6	BLACKLEG	1
SKIN COLOUR	r	COMMON SCAB	6
FLESH COLOUR	3	POWDERY SCAB	4
DRY MATTER	3	SPRAING	1
RESISTANCE TO DISCOLOURING	[6]	POTATO CYST NEMATODE	S
RESISTANCE TO DISINTEGRATION	-	SLUG	1

SHARPE'S EXPRESS

1900
First early
ENGLAND

This classic was produced by Charles Sharpe of Sleaford. He was a major miller and seedsman and it is not clear whether he was involved personally in plant breeding. 'Express' has high dry matter, very good flavour and cooks well although boiling requires care. It was TV gardener Percy Thrower's favourite. Yield and disease resistance are poor but several of Scotland's leading growers used to certify a small patch to keep the variety going for their own use.

TUBER		RESISTANCE	
YIELD	4	FOLIAR BLIGHT	4
TUBER SHAPE	7	TUBER BLIGHT	2
EYE DEPTH	[6]	BLACKLEG	-
SKIN COLOUR	w	COMMON SCAB	[3]
FLESH COLOUR	3	POWDERY SCAB	-
DRY MATTER	7	SPRAING	-
RESISTANCE TO DISCOLOURING	7	POTATO CYST NEMATODE	S
RESISTANCE TO DISINTEGRATION	3	SLUG	-

103

SHULA
1986
Early maincrop
SCOTLAND

This is another high-yielding Scottish Crops Research Institute variety with pink eyes. It is bred from 'Pentland Hawk', stores very well and has good flavour as a result. Its lack of eelworm resistance and the cooking characteristics are disappointing, but this is another variety with a small but keen following on the look-out for sources of fresh stock.

TUBER		RESISTANCE	
YIELD	7	FOLIAR BLIGHT	5
TUBER SHAPE	6	TUBER BLIGHT	6
EYE DEPTH	5	BLACKLEG	5
SKIN COLOUR	w/r	COMMON SCAB	5
FLESH COLOUR	3	POWDERY SCAB	6
DRY MATTER	6	SPRAING	I
RESISTANCE TO DISCOLOURING	4	POTATO CYST NEMATODE	S
RESISTANCE TO DISINTEGRATION	4	SLUG	5

SIERRA
1991
Early maincrop
ENGLAND

'Sierra' is a PBI Cambridge, high-yielding, processing variety. It is unusual in having some white eelworm resistance but no common yellow eelworm resistance. It is dry, floury and tasty.

TUBER		RESISTANCE	
YIELD	8	FOLIAR BLIGHT	4
TUBER SHAPE	5	TUBER BLIGHT	5
EYE DEPTH	5	BLACKLEG	I
SKIN COLOUR	y	COMMON SCAB	4
FLESH COLOUR	5	POWDERY SCAB	5
DRY MATTER	7	SPRAING	I
RESISTANCE TO DISCOLOURING	7	POTATO CYST NEMATODE	S
RESISTANCE TO DISINTEGRATION	3	SLUG	4

SLANEY
1993
Late maincrop
IRELAND

This is a high-yielding TEAGASC variety. It is an all-white boiling potato bred from 'Cara'. It is waxy if grown in the south of the UK but wet in the north.

TUBER			RESISTANCE	
YIELD	[9]		FOLIAR BLIGHT	5
TUBER SHAPE	4		TUBER BLIGHT	3
EYE DEPTH	5		BLACKLEG	4
SKIN COLOUR	w		COMMON SCAB	6
FLESH COLOUR	4		POWDERY SCAB	4
DRY MATTER	3		SPRAING	8
RESISTANCE TO DISCOLOURING	6		POTATO CYST NEMATODE	r
RESISTANCE TO DISINTEGRATION	7		SLUG	4

SPEY
1998
Late maincrop
SCOTLAND

This is another Scottish Crop Research Institute red-eyed variety with large yields. The tubers are long, and careful earthing up is important to prevent greening. It is general purpose with high enough dry matter to be used commercially for chipping. The flavour is excellent, the variety has some slug resistance and it is double eelworm resistant. This is a good garden variety.

TUBER			RESISTANCE	
YIELD	7		FOLIAR BLIGHT	5
TUBER SHAPE	7		TUBER BLIGHT	4
EYE DEPTH	6		BLACKLEG	7
SKIN COLOUR	w/r		COMMON SCAB	6
FLESH COLOUR	3		POWDERY SCAB	5
DRY MATTER	6		SPRAING	1
RESISTANCE TO DISCOLOURING	5		POTATO CYST NEMATODE	r
RESISTANCE TO DISINTEGRATION	6		SLUG	4

SPUNTA
1967
Second early
NETHERLANDS

This is best known as a Cyprus potato. 'Spunta' tubers are large, long and waxy. They cook well with a 'mild' flavour. Blight resistance is surprisingly good. Nearly all seed is exported and a small number of 'waxy' enthusiasts find it difficult to replace stock.

TUBER		RESISTANCE	
YIELD	7	FOLIAR BLIGHT	7
TUBER SHAPE	7	TUBER BLIGHT	6
EYE DEPTH	7	BLACKLEG	-
SKIN COLOUR	y	COMMON SCAB	3
FLESH COLOUR	5	POWDERY SCAB	-
DRY MATTER	2	SPRAING	4
RESISTANCE TO DISCOLOURING	7	POTATO CYST NEMATODE	s
RESISTANCE TO DISINTEGRATION	8	SLUG	[4]

STEMSTER
1986
Early maincrop
SCOTLAND

Bred by Jack Dunnett, this is a pale red maincrop which has very high yields, good disease resistance and good drought resistance. Little is grown in the UK but it has become fairly important in France. French-grown 'Stemster' seed exports exceed those of Jack's native Scotland.

TUBER		RESISTANCE	
YIELD	9	FOLIAR BLIGHT	4
TUBER SHAPE	6	TUBER BLIGHT	5
EYE DEPTH	6	BLACKLEG	6
SKIN COLOUR	r	COMMON SCAB	4
FLESH COLOUR	6	POWDERY SCAB	6
DRY MATTER	3	SPRAING	6
RESISTANCE TO DISCOLOURING	6	POTATO CYST NEMATODE	r
RESISTANCE TO DISINTEGRATION	7	SLUG	2

STIRLING
1990
Early maincrop
SCOTLAND

'Stirling' is a high-yielding Scottish Crop Research Institute variety. Its high blight resistance led to it being featured at the 1994 HDRA potato event. It has not been a commercial success – because, I believe, the flavour is exceptionally 'mild', and the variety is not eelworm resistant and prone to blackleg, spraing, hollow heart and internal rust spot.

TUBER		RESISTANCE	
YIELD	8	FOLIAR BLIGHT	8
TUBER SHAPE	5	TUBER BLIGHT	7
EYE DEPTH	7	BLACKLEG	1
SKIN COLOUR	w	COMMON SCAB	7
FLESH COLOUR	3	POWDERY SCAB	5
DRY MATTER	4	SPRAING	1
RESISTANCE TO DISCOLOURING	4	POTATO CYST NEMATODE	s
RESISTANCE TO DISINTEGRATION	4	SLUG	4

STROMA
1989
Second early
SCOTLAND

This is a red Jack Dunnett variety, named after an island off his native Caithness. It is pretty, although the colour is not as strong as showbench exhibitors like. It has quite high yields, a mild flavour and good cooking characteristics. Its disease resistance includes partial double eelworm resistance. It is rarely found in horticultural outlets and a small number of my 'waxy' friends are on a quest to change this.

TUBER		RESISTANCE	
YIELD	7	FOLIAR BLIGHT	4
TUBER SHAPE	7	TUBER BLIGHT	4
EYE DEPTH	5	BLACKLEG	8
SKIN COLOUR	r	COMMON SCAB	7
FLESH COLOUR	6	POWDERY SCAB	6
DRY MATTER	3	SPRAING	4
RESISTANCE TO DISCOLOURING	7	POTATO CYST NEMATODE	pr
RESISTANCE TO DISINTEGRATION	8	SLUG	3

SWIFT
1994
First early
SCOTLAND

The unexpected product of a Jack Dunnett 'Stroma' cross, this is white and very early. The 'bird' series name is an appropriate pun. It produces fewer, larger tubers than 'Rocket'. The foliage is short and it is one of the best varieties for growing in pots or under polythene, glass or fleece. The disease resistance is good and includes partial double eelworm resistance.

TUBER		RESISTANCE	
YIELD	8	FOLIAR BLIGHT	4
TUBER SHAPE	5	TUBER BLIGHT	3
EYE DEPTH	7	BLACKLEG	6
SKIN COLOUR	w	COMMON SCAB	7
FLESH COLOUR	6	POWDERY SCAB	5
DRY MATTER	5	SPRAING	5
RESISTANCE TO DISCOLOURING	[7]	POTATO CYST NEMATODE	pr
RESISTANCE TO DISINTEGRATION	[6]	SLUG	-

SYMFONIA
1994
Early maincrop
NETHERLANDS

'Symfonia' is an unusual, high dry matter, red-skinned Dutch variety with good disease resistance, which may be pretty enough for showing. Its blight resistance is quite good and sometimes organic seed is available.

TUBER		RESISTANCE	
YIELD	6	FOLIAR BLIGHT	8
TUBER SHAPE	6	TUBER BLIGHT	4
EYE DEPTH	6	BLACKLEG	2
SKIN COLOUR	r	COMMON SCAB	8
FLESH COLOUR	6	POWDERY SCAB	5
DRY MATTER	8	SPRAING	8
RESISTANCE TO DISCOLOURING	[5]	POTATO CYST NEMATODE	r
RESISTANCE TO DISINTEGRATION	[4]	SLUG	3

ULSTER CHIEFTAIN

1938
First early
NORTHERN IRELAND

This variety was bred by John Clarke of Co. Antrim, who produced the famous 'Ulster' series. Only a few of the earlies, of which 'Ulster Chieftain' is the oldest, are still available. It is at its best when harvested as early as possible and is short enough to be grown under glass or polythene. It has a reputation for slug resistance.

TUBER		RESISTANCE	
YIELD	4	FOLIAR BLIGHT	3
TUBER SHAPE	4	TUBER BLIGHT	3
EYE DEPTH	[6]	BLACKLEG	-
SKIN COLOUR	w	COMMON SCAB	6
FLESH COLOUR	l	POWDERY SCAB	-
DRY MATTER	4	SPRAING	8
RESISTANCE TO DISCOLOURING	7	POTATO CYST NEMATODE	S
RESISTANCE TO DISINTEGRATION	7	SLUG	-

ULSTER PRINCE

1947
First early
NORTHERN IRELAND

This is another John Clarke variety which should be eaten as early as possible. It was the earliest early at the time it appeared and was a regional favourite in north-west England. It has good drought resistance.

TUBER		RESISTANCE	
YIELD	6	FOLIAR BLIGHT	4
TUBER SHAPE	6	TUBER BLIGHT	3
EYE DEPTH	[6]	BLACKLEG	4
SKIN COLOUR	w	COMMON SCAB	5
FLESH COLOUR	2	POWDERY SCAB	6
DRY MATTER	3	SPRAING	2
RESISTANCE TO DISCOLOURING	6	POTATO CYST NEMATODE	S
RESISTANCE TO DISINTEGRATION	9	SLUG	-

ULSTER SCEPTRE
1963
First early
NORTHERN IRELAND

This was John Clarke's most successful variety. Like the other 'Ulster's still available, it is best eaten early and fresh. The yield of waxy tubers is high, even by present standards.

TUBER		RESISTANCE	
YIELD	7	FOLIAR BLIGHT	4
TUBER SHAPE	6	TUBER BLIGHT	2
EYE DEPTH	6	BLACKLEG	4
SKIN COLOUR	w	COMMON SCAB	5
FLESH COLOUR	2	POWDERY SCAB	6
DRY MATTER	3	SPRAING	3
RESISTANCE TO DISCOLOURING	7	POTATO CYST NEMATODE	S
RESISTANCE TO DISINTEGRATION	8	SLUG	-

UP TO DATE
1894
Late maincrop
SCOTLAND

This is an Archibald Findlay classic which was exported worldwide. Its existence started the export trade in Scottish seed. This was the first Cyprus potato in the early years and was the main variety in the UK and the then British Empire for decades. Its late-maturing foliage (which is spectacular) and its susceptibility to blight can cause problems but large crops of quality waxy tubers are possible.

TUBER		RESISTANCE	
YIELD	5	FOLIAR BLIGHT	2
TUBER SHAPE	5	TUBER BLIGHT	4
EYE DEPTH	7	BLACKLEG	-
SKIN COLOUR	w	COMMON SCAB	4
FLESH COLOUR	3	POWDERY SCAB	-
DRY MATTER	5	SPRAING	-
RESISTANCE TO DISCOLOURING	-	POTATO CYST NEMATODE	S
RESISTANCE TO DISINTEGRATION	7	SLUG	-

VALOR

1993
Late maincrop
SCOTLAND

This is another Jack Dunnett waxy variety. Organic farmers picked it up first but now other growers are looking at it as a means of coping with low prices. 'Mild' flavoured, it requires relatively low inputs, can produce high yields on second-choice, cheaper land, is very disease resistant (double eelworm resistant) and needs less spraying than some varieties.

TUBER		RESISTANCE	
YIELD	8	FOLIAR BLIGHT	5
TUBER SHAPE	5	TUBER BLIGHT	7
EYE DEPTH	5	BLACKLEG	4
SKIN COLOUR	w	COMMON SCAB	5
FLESH COLOUR	2	POWDERY SCAB	5
DRY MATTER	2	SPRAING	6
RESISTANCE TO DISCOLOURING	6	POTATO CYST NEMATODE	r
RESISTANCE TO DISINTEGRATION	5	SLUG	4

VANESSA

1973
First early
NETHERLANDS

'Vanessa' is very like an early 'Desiree' but the tubers tend to be smoother and more suitable for exhibition use. Even the foliage is very 'Desiree'-like.

TUBER		RESISTANCE	
YIELD	[7]	FOLIAR BLIGHT	[4]
TUBER SHAPE	6	TUBER BLIGHT	[2]
EYE DEPTH	6	BLACKLEG	[2]
SKIN COLOUR	r	COMMON SCAB	[5]
FLESH COLOUR	5	POWDERY SCAB	-
DRY MATTER	[4]	SPRAING	[4]
RESISTANCE TO DISCOLOURING	[7]	POTATO CYST NEMATODE	s
RESISTANCE TO DISINTEGRATION	[8]	SLUG	-

VERITY
1998
Late maincrop
SCOTLAND

This was released by Jack Dunnett with organic growing in mind because of its disease resistance. It is red eyed and is supposed to have the disease resistance of 'Cara' and the eating quality of 'King Edward', although it is not related to either. In my growing conditions I have not experienced 'King Edward'-type eating quality with this variety. Lack of eelworm resistance is a problem.

TUBER		RESISTANCE	
YIELD	[8]	FOLIAR BLIGHT	[8]
TUBER SHAPE	5	TUBER BLIGHT	[7]
EYE DEPTH	7	BLACKLEG	7
SKIN COLOUR	w/r	COMMON SCAB	5
FLESH COLOUR	3	POWDERY SCAB	6
DRY MATTER	7	SPRAING	-
RESISTANCE TO DISCOLOURING	7	POTATO CYST NEMATODE	s
RESISTANCE TO DISINTEGRATION	-	SLUG	-

VICTORIA
c.2000
Early maincrop
NETHERLANDS

This is not the famous variety of 1863 bred by William Paterson and named after a certain queen. Nearly all the classic varieties of breeders such as Nicol, Clark, Penn and Findlay had the 1863 'Victoria' in their parentage. I can't bear to promote this new chipping variety, presumably named after Mrs Beckham (I hope I'm wrong). Please use the ratings and judge for yourself.

TUBER		RESISTANCE	
YIELD	6	FOLIAR BLIGHT	4
TUBER SHAPE	6	TUBER BLIGHT	3
EYE DEPTH	6	BLACKLEG	6
SKIN COLOUR	y	COMMON SCAB	5
FLESH COLOUR	7	POWDERY SCAB	4
DRY MATTER	[5]	SPRAING	4
RESISTANCE TO DISCOLOURING	-	POTATO CYST NEMATODE	r
RESISTANCE TO DISINTEGRATION	-	SLUG	5

WHITE LADY
1999
Late maincrop
HUNGARY

This variety was produced by a university in Hungary. It was taken up originally because of its high blight resistance but this has been overcome to some extent by the evolving fungus. It has been revived, in the case of garden use at least, because of good reports on flavour.

TUBER		RESISTANCE	
YIELD	-	FOLIAR BLIGHT	[5]
TUBER SHAPE	[5]	TUBER BLIGHT	[5]
EYE DEPTH	[7]	BLACKLEG	[3]
SKIN COLOUR	w	COMMON SCAB	[6]
FLESH COLOUR	[2]	POWDERY SCAB	-
DRY MATTER	[7]	SPRAING	-
RESISTANCE TO DISCOLOURING	-	POTATO CYST NEMATODE	r
RESISTANCE TO DISINTEGRATION	-	SLUG	-

WILJA
1967
Second early
NETHERLANDS

In the 1970s, 'Wilja', along with 'Estima', changed all the rules about growing second earlies. High yields, good appearance, good boiling qualities and easily managed foliage proved to be more important than disease resistance, white flesh and floury flavour.

TUBER		RESISTANCE	
YIELD	7	FOLIAR BLIGHT	3
TUBER SHAPE	7	TUBER BLIGHT	5
EYE DEPTH	7	BLACKLEG	5
SKIN COLOUR	y	COMMON SCAB	7
FLESH COLOUR	5	POWDERY SCAB	5
DRY MATTER	4	SPRAING	5
RESISTANCE TO DISCOLOURING	7	POTATO CYST NEMATODE	s
RESISTANCE TO DISINTEGRATION	8	SLUG	5

WINSTON

1992
First early
SCOTLAND

'Winston' is a smooth, bold, Jack Dunnett variety. It is one of the first bakers of the season. It has disease resistance and is among the most successful showbench varieties of all time.

TUBER		RESISTANCE	
YIELD	8	FOLIAR BLIGHT	5
TUBER SHAPE	5	TUBER BLIGHT	5
EYE DEPTH	6	BLACKLEG	4
SKIN COLOUR	w	COMMON SCAB	5
FLESH COLOUR	4	POWDERY SCAB	6
DRY MATTER	2	SPRAING	5
RESISTANCE TO DISCOLOURING	8	POTATO CYST NEMATODE	-
RESISTANCE TO DISINTEGRATION	4	SLUG	-

YUKON GOLD

1980
Second early
CANADA

This is a very attractive, bold, yellow baker. It stands out visually from other varieties and is said to have a buttery flavour. It has moderately high dry matter and fries well. It has surprisingly good boiling qualities. There is some *Solanum phureja* in the background breeding.

TUBER		RESISTANCE	
YIELD	4	FOLIAR BLIGHT	3
TUBER SHAPE	4	TUBER BLIGHT	3
EYE DEPTH	7	BLACKLEG	5
SKIN COLOUR	y	COMMON SCAB	4
FLESH COLOUR	6	POWDERY SCAB	4
DRY MATTER	6	SPRAING	2
RESISTANCE TO DISCOLOURING	8	POTATO CYST NEMATODE	s
RESISTANCE TO DISINTEGRATION	7	SLUG	4

VARIETIES THAT MAY BE AVAILABLE AS MICROPLANTS

A variety has to be on the National List or the EU Common Catalogue of Varieties before it can be sold legally as certified seed. I (and, subsequently, companies I have been associated with) have been allowed to arrange for microplants to be produced of other varieties, mainly heritage, to be sold through catalogues in the UK. This started when it seemed that the EU was about to introduce legislation to allow the use of local traditional varieties of vegetables outwith the very expensive and complicated regime of the Common Catalogue. This has not happened and although it is recognized that one of the aims of the National Collection is to keep old varieties for posterity and that disease-free microplants cannot be a threat to field crop health, the permission to produce microplants could be withdrawn at any time. The varieties involved, therefore, have a different status from those in the main guide, require different growing techniques (see page 29) and are generally more expensive.

AMERICA
1876

Better known as 'Irish Cobbler' in its native USA, this is a spontaneous white sport of Albert Bresee's pink 'Early Rose', which was said to have been found in the garden of an Irish cobbler in Marblehead, Massachusetts. It is round with white, waxy flesh. This was probably the first white first early to reach Europe.

ARRAN COMRADE
1918

This is a round, smooth, white second early selected by Donald Mackelvie on Arran from seed supplied by F.W. Keay of Merry Hill, Wolverhampton. It has recently been revived at the request of showbench enthusiasts. Several were of the opinion that it outclassed modern favourites as far as their requirements for a round white variety were concerned. Time will tell. The variety also had a great reputation for excellent flavour and good cooking characteristics. It is susceptible to blight but at its peak it was regarded as a vigorous, reliable cropper.

AURA
1951

'Aura' is a second early, long, yellow, salad type from France. It was sold by a UK mail-order catalogue and when it was dropped it was kept going by enthusiasts. Tubers were donated to the Henry Doubleday Research Association's Heritage Seed Library. It was rated highly by the members for flavour and cooking characteristics. When increasing blight pressure forced HDRA to stop keeping potatoes, I initiated the process which led to it being available as a microplant.

THE BISHOP
1912

This relatively low-yielding, late maincrop was produced by Dr. J.H. Wilson of St Andrews University. It is of interest because several exhibitors are of the opinion that it is the best long, white kidney available for late shows. (The term 'kidney' has fallen out of use except among exhibitors. It means 'oval', or sometimes 'flattened oval'.) It is certainly very attractive and the virus-free stock now available has led to the production of tubers large enough for the showbench for the first time in many years. The tubers are firm and waxy and store well.

BLUE KESTREL
1996

This is my tiny contribution to the world of potatoes. I found the first tuber while hand lifting a small organic seed crop of 'Kestrel' at Berryhill Farm near Newburgh, Fife. 'Blue Kestrel' is an all, or almost all, blue sport of 'Kestrel'. The foliage, eating qualities and yield are very similar to those of ordinary blue-eyed 'Kestrel'. As with most coloured sports, some of the tubers revert back to something like the original after a few garden-grown generations. I have been delighted to spot it occasionally at shows.

BUTE BLUES
before 1923

Catalogues chose this blue-skinned variety from the National Collection because the name appeals. Islands are always interesting and the extra, unnecessary 's' makes it very 'rock 'n' roll'.

There is an interesting history of plant breeding on Bute. New varieties of dahlias, pansies, roses, sweet peas and many other flowers and some vegetables were bred by Dobbie and Co. when the company was on Bute from 1875 to 1910, the year it became Messrs Dobbie and Co. of Edinburgh. The residence of the Marquis of Bute, Mount Stewart, has one of the finest gardens in the country and in the later Victorian era employed a very large gardening staff.

Tracing the history of the 'Bute' varieties has proved to be very frustrating. My main source was Salaman, the great 'sorter' of potato chaos. I started by assuming there was some Bute connection between 'Bute Blues', 'Beauty of Bute', 'Pride of Bute' and 'Marquis of Bute'. These are all separate varieties with distinct characteristics kept in the National Collection. 'Beauty of Bute' was said to have been raised by James Heron of 'Rothsea', Bute. The museum at Rothesay could find no trace of the activities of this gentleman and he did not appear in any census around that time. 'Marquis of Bute' was raised on Arran by Donald Mackelvie. The Marquis was described to me as the 'Bill Gates of his day' because he owned so many coal mines and he had fame well beyond the Clyde. Salaman dismisses 'Pride of Bute' as a synonym of 'Surprise', a variety of unknown history. To add to my confusion a variety called 'Bute Blue', without the sexy 's', is also an alternative name for 'Surprise'. 'Bute Boys' and 'Bute Mary' are also recorded by Salaman as synonyms of other varieties.

The Bute connection is unproven but 'Bute Blues' is early maincrop, blue skinned and white fleshed – floury and tasty.

CHAMPION
1876

It took John Nicol of Arbroath some time to introduce his famous 'Champion', which went on to be the most common variety in Ireland for several decades. It is a late maincrop which produces white tubers with perhaps a purple blush at the stolon end. They are floury, yellow fleshed and of legendary flavour. The tubers have long dormancy and the microplants are slow to start. The legendary status of 'Champion' in Ireland is reflected in the Irish surnames of many microplant customers.

CONGO
before 1895

This is sometimes known as 'Blue Congo', 'Black Congo' or 'Purple Congo' or rather confusingly as 'Himalayan Black'. It is famous for having dark blue/purple skin with bright blue flesh which intensifies with maturity. The tubers develop very late in the season and are often small and cylindrical with blunt ends and many eyes. It is recorded as being British in origin and somewhere I have picked up that it was possibly a Border shepherds' potato. It was grown as a novelty salad potato on a very small scale. It does not have a great reputation for flavour or yield. One of the largest potato companies in the UK grew some recently in Finland to provide the raw material to make novelty crisps which were sold through the farm shops

belonging to the royal family. They were surprisingly good. This would indicate that it is a high dry matter type not suited to the modern concept of a salad.

EDGCOTE PURPLE
before 1916

I should not really include this one because I don't think that I have actually arranged for the variety to be micropropagated, but I have been meaning to do so for some years.

It is another variety at the centre of a small piece of social history. It was raised by Mr Wilde of Edgcote and had a small commercial success in Wiltshire where, over many years, it showed great resistance to virus and had a great reputation for quality. It is a vigorous early maincrop with very dark purple skin and pale yellow flesh. It still has a fine reputation, perhaps indirectly, for flavour and cooking characteristics.

In neighbouring Gloucestershire a variety called 'Gloucester Black Kidney' has the same reputation. It is said to have been looted from a train crash which was famous for its high death toll and the apocryphal story of a dead child who was never identified. It is difficult to believe that someone would steal potatoes to grow from such a situation but the word-of-mouth story still persists in the locality generations later.

In at least one Cotswold village the residents claim to have their own version of 'Black Kidney', different from that of Gloucester. In South Wales a friend still exhibits his favourite, beautifully named, black kidney, 'Port Wine Kidney'. He also shows 'Gloucester Black Kidney' and 'Edgcote Purple'. However, according to Redcliffe Salaman, 'Gloucester Black Kidney' and 'Port Wine Kidney' are synonyms of 'Edgcote Purple', which he used extensively in crosses while studying the genetics of potatoes. DNA testing would tell the true story.

FLOURBALL
1895

'Flourball' is an early maincrop pink/red produced by Miss King of Mount Mellick in Ireland and marketed through Suttons. It is round, white fleshed, floury and very tasty. It was a parent of several of the 'Arran' varieties.

FORTYFOLD
before 1836

This is one of the oldest varieties still in collection. It is a late maincrop. It is mentioned in Victorian literature as being an old type with famously high yields. The massive number of tubers grow closely together on short stolons at the bottom of the plant. They vary greatly in size, many of them being small, and they can be difficult to harvest commercially. The crop in terms of weight is quite prodigious even by modern standards. The tubers are round, deep eyed and purple with white splashes. They have a pleasant nutty flavour and a texture that is very different from that of modern varieties. It is said to come originally from Lancashire and was a parent of 'Kerr's Pink'. The original version was said to be red. It is noticeable in the field that colour intensity and distribution is very variable.

There was the possibility of an intriguing link with the Canary Islands. Some years ago, my friend Alan Wilson, who is also a potato enthusiast (and author of a very good book on potatoes), mentioned that he had been to the Canary Islands on potato business and had been shown the old variety used extensively in traditional cooking. He was fairly certain that it was the same as 'Fortyfold' and therefore British in origin. I had recently learned that 'Fortyfold' had been grown continuously for many generations on Orkney. Its possible widespread use after such a long time was interesting enough for us to look into the variety and

we were then involved in introducing it into the Waitrose heritage range.

A few years later, I was on duty at the Chelsea Flower Show with the Three Countries Potato Group display when we were approached by some people from the Canary Islands. They enjoyed the display of several hundred potatoes and mentioned that their traditional variety, which has a red as well as a purple version, was reputed to have been given to the island of Tenerife by Admiral Nelson at the time of the Battle of Tenerife. I recently obtained a sample from Tenerife and persuaded the wonderful staff at the Scottish Agricultural Science Agency to compare its DNA profile with that of 'Fortyfold'. The result showed no obvious connection and a potentially good story no longer existed!

HIGHLAND BURGUNDY RED

'Highland Burgundy Red' is an almost all-red, long-tubered, maincrop variety very like some of the really old types still grown in South America. The central pith tissue is a bright burgundy colour with a very narrow white cortex band surrounding it. The skin is bright red when freshly dug but becomes more russet with underlying burgundy when it sets. Much of the colour remains when the tubers are cooked, particularly if they are steamed or fried. The cooked potato is fluffy in texture and can have a slightly sweet flavour. 'Highland Burgundy Red' looks as if it should be suitable for salad use but the variety has high dry matter and makes excellent novelty crisps, chips and mash.

I have to confess to a probable mistake when I was involved in reviving this variety. I was approached at the East Anglian Potato Event by Gordon and Sue Baldam, then of Nordelph, Norfolk, who gave me my first, very sickly, tuber. They had been given the variety by friends who had received it from Mr Harris, an elderly HDRA member. He, in turn, had obtained it in the early 1970s from the eighty-year-old grandson of a former Royal Botanic Gardens, Kew curator. There is supposed to be a newspaper clipping in existence which tells of the variety being used in 1936 for a special dinner at the Savoy in honour of the Duke of Burgundy. This is convoluted but believable partial provenance for the name anyway.

Gordon and Sue were a little annoyed when the HDRA Heritage Seed Library turned the variety down on the grounds that it was the same as 'Red Salad', a variety in the Donald Maclean Collection at Crieff. I had only seen a photograph of 'Red Salad' and, with hindsight, it was probably a cooked tuber because the internal red colouring seemed to be continuous. I arranged for 'Highland Burgandy Red' to be micropropagated and cleaned of its heavy virus content, confident that it was different. It was placed in the disease-free *in vitro* part of the National Collection. 'Red Salad' had come and gone, possibly more than once, in the field-grown part of the National Collection.

I became worried a year or two ago when I found one cut sample of 'Red Salad' after another seemed to have the white cortex band in the tuber just like 'Highland Burgundy Red'. I grew samples of the two nominally different varieties and, in all cases, the foliage and flowers were very similar. I am suspicious now that 'Red Salad', along with the 'Beetroot Tattie' of Caithness and 'Egyptian Red' of another collection, is the same as 'Highland Burgandy Red'. This is another example where DNA profiling might cast some light on potato confusion. I had at first assumed that the 'Egyptian Red' name indicated it was the product of some modern dubious smuggling but in fact 'Egyptian' is an old term for Romany gypsy and was often applied to anything exotic and colourful.

KEPPLESTONE KIDNEY
before 1919

This is an old, blue-skinned, early maincrop with light yellow flesh. It has a long oval tuber, more pointed at one end. It was often known as the 'Ram's Horn'. An elderly worthy told me that a variety of this name was an old favourite for flavour in my Fife village for years before its eventual extinction.

The name 'Kepplestone' has always seemed familiar. I realized recently that it was because Kepplestone was the destination of the buses of my childhood in Aberdeenshire.

LORD ROSEBERY
before 1920

This round, red, second early has floury, white, tasty flesh. It was probably produced by garden staff at Dalmeny Estate, the home of Lord Rosebery, near South Queensferry just to the west of Edinburgh. (Salaman lists 'Dalmeny Early Queen' as a distinct variety and nine other 'Dalmeny' varieties as mere synonyms of others.)

MEIN'S EARLY ROUND
1916

This is a round to short oval, white, second early with striking deep red eyes. The flesh is white with a pleasant flavour. Salaman lists three other 'Mein's' varieties as being mere synonyms. I have been told by folk attending the Borders Potato Event that there is word-of-mouth evidence that Mr Mein was a potato breeder from Roxburgh before the First World War.

MR BRESEE
around 1870

This variety was raised by Albert Bresee of Habbardson, Vermont, of 'Early Rose' fame. Bresee was one of the leading members of the American group of plant breeders who introduced real earliness and prettiness into potato varieties. 'Mr Bresee' (the potato) is a second early pink/red with flattened oval tubers which have an almost translucent quality. The flesh is white and waxy and was described at the time as insipid, soapy and moist. Nowadays it would be described as a salad type, pleasant when eaten fresh! The variety was very successful on the showbench in the early part of the twentieth century. Recent trials with a view to introducing it into supermarkets as a heritage punnet variety were not successful, I suspect because the name, price and concept left potential customers bewildered. The trials showed, however, that the variety completely outyielded 'Maris Peer' grown in the same field.

ORION
1947

'Orion' was bred by Dr T.P. McIntosh, who was in charge of the very important potato section of the Department of Agriculture in Scotland. He also bred the famous variety 'Dr McIntosh' and developed much of the modern seed potato regime we know today. He was a hard and energetic taskmaster and I have met several elderly gentlemen who, as young potato inspectors, found life demanding under Dr McIntosh. 'Orion' is an early maincrop. The tubers are round oval with white skin and pale yellow flesh. It was said by Lawrence Hills, the founder of HDRA, to be the smoothest mashing potato known. It has a very distinctive white flower with holes between the fused petals.

PEACHBLOOM
before 1923

This is a round, late maincrop, part red-coloured with deep eyes. It is American and probably dates from the period between the 1850s and the 1880s when there was a great profusion of such varieties. It may well be the same variety as 'Peachblow'. introduced by B.K. Bliss and Sons into Britain in 1881. The flesh is white and is said to be tender and sweet. The variety is of interest because the skin surface has a remarkable bloom or shine.

PINK DUKE OF YORK
before 1956

This is a delicate pink sport of the very well-known classic first early which was first placed in the National Collection in 1956. When I was young, only the very keenest potato enthusiast had this variety. It was very rare and could be obtained only from other enthusiasts. Its rarity may well have fuelled its strong reputation for being a culinary improvement on the already very fine white 'Duke of York'.

PURPLE EYED SEEDLING
1970s

There have been several 'Purple Eyed Seedlings' in the past. This one is said to have originated in the University of Wales, Aberystwyth. It is a very pretty oval potato with bright patches of purple rather like 'Kestrel' but with pale yellow flesh. This is the 'pet' potato of Bill Hughes of Swansea, who has used it in his collection on six occasions to win the British Potato Championship. It became so infected with virus that he could no longer produce large tubers and asked me if it could be cleaned up and micropropagated.

SALAD BLUE

This is a mystery on top of an enigma. It is a vigorous early maincrop which produces lots of useful-looking, all-blue, oval tubers. It is much more productive than the other well-known all-blue variety, 'Congo'. It is not a salad potato for it has high dry matter and produces excellent deep blue novelty crisps, chips and mash.

The red, purple and blue pigments in potatoes are anthocyanins which are antioxidants. They are completely tasteless but have strong anticarcinogen properties. I sometimes wonder if the colour in novelty crisps balances the harm that the frying process does.

The 'Salad Blue' flowers are very distinctive. They are strong with white and blue/purple petals and yellow anthers which turn black, presumably when the unusually dark pollen is released.

I am mystified about the origins of this variety. It has not been in the National Collection until recently and is not mentioned by Salaman. It is spread widely among enthusiasts who have grown it for years. It

seems to originate from the Maclean Collection. There are several varieties in America such as 'All Blue' and 'Californian Blue' which have similar tubers. I am suspicious that the name is descriptive rather than authentic. The fly in the ointment is that the people reclaiming the Lost Gardens of Heligan found an old Victorian cast-lead plant label for 'Salad Blue' and have made much of it, assuming it was this potato which they now grow extensively.

SHERINE
1987

This is often described as a 'sister' variety of 'Nadine'. Like 'Nadine', 'Sherine' was bred in 1987 by Jack Dunnett and it is also an oval second early with white skin and cream flesh. I know nothing of its disease resistance but it is usually very attractive – indeed several exhibitors prefer it to 'Nadine'. Jack saw little point in having two similar varieties competing with each other in a very tight market and withdrew 'Sherine' from national listing but not before he had generously given several samples to keen exhibitors. Their progeny are still winning rosettes to this day but the time has come for this stock to be replaced by virus-free microplants. With

the approval of Jack Dunnett, 'Sherine' microplants are becoming available.

SHETLAND BLACK
before 1923

Many on Shetland would like to think that this striking variety was salvaged from a sunken Armada ship of 1588. It is a second early which produces lots of small to medium, oval, netted tubers. The skin is very dark blue to the point of appearing black and the eyes are shallow. Inside, the flesh is pale yellow and floury with a very distinctive purple vascular ring. The tubers are very tasty, high dry matter crofter fuel. Their earliness, combined with their high yield and the shallow nature of the eyes, indicates that they have American 'Early Rose' genes in them. This would make them late Victorian at the earliest. This rather spoils the romance of the Armada story. There are many on Shetland, however, who don't think the National Collection version of the variety is 'right'. The authentic version is supposed to be larger, round with deep eyes and late, but still with the distinctive purple vascular ring. I don't know about the maturity characteristics but I have seen just such a tuber labelled 'Orkney Black' in a private collection. Another case for genetic profilers to have fun with.

SKERRY BLUE
before 1846

This is an old, late maincrop from Ireland which pre-dates the famine. It is low yielding but of high quality with very high dry matter. Its short oval tubers have blue skin and cream flesh. It is important historically because it was said to be the only variety with enough blight resistance to grow in the famine years. Unfortunately, very few possessed tubers because everyone relied on high-yielding 'Lumpers'.

Several years ago an elderly gentleman, originally from Donegal, tracked me down and phoned to offer me his stock of 'Skerry Blue' for posterity. I'm afraid I did not know enough to be excited and refused it, explaining that the variety had long been safely in the National Collection but that I would be interested in any anecdotal history. He told me that when he left school, well before the Second World War, he migrated to Argyll to become a jobbing gardener. There he learned about the qualities of the legendary 'Skerry Blue' from Irish gardeners in that area and was told that it had been the custom since the 1870s to bring some tubers of this variety over from Ireland to grow for personal consumption in Argyll. He was determined to grow them in his garden. He eventually tracked some down, presumably late in the planting season, for the only material available was already growing out of a half-rotten 'blight midden'. He kept the variety going from this unpromising start for more than sixty years. I am left with the strong feeling that I did not do the right thing.

WITCHHILL
1881?

This was originally the variety 'Snowdrop' reputedly produced by Mr Cole somewhere in the English Midlands. The stock that was first released was very diverse, to the point that it may have been a mixture of seed-produced varieties. Messrs Dobbie and Co. of Edinburgh may have selected a consistent, attractive, early, white-fleshed version to fit the 'Snowdrop' name and from this selection Alex Brown of Witchhill, Fraserburgh possibly reselected or bred 'Witchhill'. The dates involved are confusing and this is only one version of events.

Brown's 'Witchhill' is the selection available to posterity in the National Collection. The variety is important historically because 'Snowdrop' was the first variety to be identified as having immunity to the devastating wart disease and many subsequent immune varieties have 'Snowdrop' in their breeding.

I picked it for micropropagation because it excited friends who had worked on the National Collection. It was very good to eat and, when it was totally cleaned of all virus, possibly for the first time in its history, it turned out to be extremely vigorous and high yielding. It is on the boundary of the first early and second early definitions and has trial yields to match any modern variety in the same category.

YETHOLM GYPSY (MR LITTLE'S)
date unknown

This was sent to me by two Scottish shepherds, Matthew and William Little of Yetholm, after I met them at the Scottish Borders Potato Event in 1998. It was cleared of virus in Edinburgh and turned out to be the only known variety to show red, white and blue colour together in the skin. As the tuber grows the attractive blue/purple outer pigment layer can give way at random to show a white and part red layer underneath. It is an early maincrop with medium-sized tubers and a pleasant, fairly dry, cream flesh.

The Little family had been given their original tubers by a friend at the first Yetholm Fair to be held after the Second World War. It was thought to be old then. The fair was a traditional gypsy horse fair, for Town Yetholm and Kirk Yetholm are among the few places in Scotland to have had a very strong link with Romany gypsies. A tiny pink cottage in Kirk Yetholm is called the Gypsy Palace and it was here in 1899, accompanied by media attention, that the king of the gypsies was crowned. My suspicion is that the potato dates from about that time and was produced by a local hobby breeder. All concerned in marketing microplants have agreed to call the variety 'Mr Little's Yetholm Gypsy' as a mark of respect for the now-deceased William Little.

SELECT BIBLIOGRAPHY

British Potato Council, *The British Seed Potato Variety Handbook*, BPC 2000

Cox, A.E., *The Potato: a Practical and Scientific Guide*, W.H. & L. Collingridge 1967

Dept. of Agriculture and Fisheries for Scotland, *Seed Potatoes: the Maintenance of Pure, Healthy and Vigorous Stocks*, HMSO Edinburgh 1966

Dept. of Agriculture for Scotland, *Report on the Marketing of Potatoes in Scotland*, HMSO Edinburgh 1933

Dunnett, Jack, *A Scottish Potato Breeder's Harvest*, North of Scotland Newspapers 2000

Findlay, Archibald, *The Potato: its History and Culture*, Archibald Findlay 1905

Graulich, David, *The French Fry Companion*, Lebhar-Friedman Books 1999

Hills, Lawrence D., *Grow Your Own Fruit and Vegetables*, Faber and Faber 1971

Kime, T., *The Great Potato Boom*, T. Kime *c.*1917

MacDonald, Douglas M., *A Classification of Potato Varieties in the Reference Collection at East Craigs, Edinburgh*, Scottish Office Agriculture and Fisheries Department 1991

Ministry of Agriculture, Fisheries and Food, various ADAS advisory leaflets on potato growing and potato diseases, HMSO various dates

National Institute of Agricultural Botany, *Potato Diseases*, NIAB and PMB

National Institute of Agricultural Botany, *Potato Variety Handbook*, NIAB 1992–2004

NIVAA and RIVRO, *Netherlands Catalogue of Potato Varieties*, NIVAA and RIVRO 1980 and 1982, and NIVAA 1997

Potato Marketing Board, *British Atlas of Potato Varieties*, PMB 1965

Potato Marketing Board, *Historical Notes on Potato Culture and Marketing* (collected by James E. Rennie), PMB 1968

Rhoades, Robert E., 'The Incredible Potato', *National Geographic,* May 1982

Romans, Alan, *Guide to Seed Potato Varieties*, Alan Romans *c.*1995 ongoing

Salaman, Redcliffe, *Potato Varieties*, Cambridge University Press 1926

Salaman, Redcliffe, *The History and Social Influence of the Potato,* Cambridge University Press 1949 (with useful update by J.G. Hawkes within editions from 1985)

Scottish Agricultural Colleges, *Potato Varieties*, SAC Guides 1980–84

Scottish Seed Potato Development Council, *Scotland: the Natural Home of Seed Potatoes*, SSPDC 1995

Whitehead T., McIntosh T. and Findlay W., *The Potato in Health and Disease*, Oliver and Boyd 1945

Wilson, Alan, *The Story of the Potato Through Illustrated Varieties*, Alan Wilson 1993

Woolfe, Jennifer A., *The Potato in the Human Diet*, Cambridge University Press 1987

Zuckerman, Larry, *The Potato: from the Andes in the Sixteenth Century to Fish and Chips, the Story of How a Vegetable Changed History*, Macmillan 1999

SUPPLIERS AND POTATO EVENTS

These suppliers have either a large range of varieties or a history of introducing new varieties. All have undertaken to supply only seed from countries free from endemic brown rot and ring rot.

MAIL ORDER
www.alanromans.com (Internet catalogue)
Thompson & Morgan 01473 688821
Mr Fothergill's Seeds 01638 552512
D.T. Brown & Co. 0845 601 4656
Suttons 01803 696363
Samuel Dobie & Son 01803 696444
Chase Organics 0845 130 1304
S.E. Marshall & Co. 01945 583407
Morrice & Anne Innes 01651 862333
Castlemill Seed Potatoes 01764 662930

GARDEN CENTRES
RHS Garden Shop, Wisley 01483 211113
Bridgend Garden Centre, Freuchie, Fife
  01337 858293

POTATO EVENTS
HDRA Ryton Gardens, Coventry (last weekend
  January/perhaps very early February)
  02476 303517
East Anglia – HDRA local groups (about the
  second Saturday in February) 01787 375153
West Yorkshire Organic Group, Shipley College
  (about the third Saturday in February)
  01274 580119
Border Organic Gardeners, Borders College,
  Galasheils (first Sunday in March) 01450 860291

ACKNOWLEDGMENTS

Much of my life has been a quest for information on potato varieties. I would like to acknowledge the help given to me over the years by nearly every potato company and potato organization in Scotland and a large number in the rest of the UK as well. With few exceptions, staff have been unstinting with their time and have given me accurate information without condition. I particularly want to thank the Scottish Agricultural Science Agency, especially Sandra Goodfellow; those at the National Institute of Agricultural Botany who gave me permission to use their 1–9 scale; and Colin Randel, first with Mr Fothergill's then with Thompson & Morgan. I greatly miss the late Bill Cuthill of Easter Kincaple farm, St Andrews, and Specialist Potatoes Ltd, who was the first to encourage me. A huge thank-you is due to four people who loaned me my main references, many of which I had sought for years: Andrew McQueen of the Three Countries Potato Group, John Nicoll of Frances Lincoln, and John Marshall and Joe Swinton of WCF Phoenix Seed Potatoes. Thanks, Mag, for everything.